Home Vegetable Gardening

Home Vegetable Gardening

A Complete and Practical Guide
to the Planting and Care of all
Vegetables, Fruits and Berries
Worth Growing for Home Use

F. F. Rockwell

Cedar Lake Classics

Copyright © 2023 by Cedar Lake Classics

This is a proofread and newly designed edition of a public domain work.

CONTENTS

Part 1

| Preface — 2

Chapter 1 | Introduction — 3

Chapter 2 | Why You Should Garden — 6

Chapter 3 | Requisites of the Home Vegetable Garden — 8

Chapter 4 | The Planting Plan — 13

Chapter 5 | Implements and Their Uses — 27

Chapter 6 | Manures and Fertilizers — 39

Chapter 7 | The Soil and Its Preparation — 55

Part 2

Vegetables

Chapter 8 | Starting the Plants — 64

Chapter 9 | Sowing and Planting — 82

CONTENTS

Chapter 10 ▎ The Cultivation of Vegetables 94

Chapter 11 ▎ The Vegetables and Their Special Needs 101

Chapter 12 ▎ Best Varieties of the Vegetable Garden 130

Chapter 13 ▎ Insects, Diseases and How to Fight Them 146

Chapter 14 ▎ Harvesting and Storing 157

Part 3

Fruits and Berries

Chapter 15 ▎ The Varieties of Pome and Stone Fruits 168

Chapter 16 ▎ Planting: Cultivation for Filler Tops 181

Chapter 17 ▎ Pruning, Spraying, and Harvesting 188

Chapter 18 ▎ Berries and Small Fruits 203

Chapter 19 ▎ A Calendar of Operations 223

Chapter 20 ▎ Conclusion 232

Part 1

Preface

With some, the home vegetable garden is a hobby; with others, especially in these days of high prices, a great help. There are many in both classes whose experience in gardening has been restricted within very narrow bounds, and whose present spare time for gardening is limited. It is as "first aid" to such persons, who want to do practical, efficient gardening, and do it with the least possible fuss and loss of time, that this book is written. In his own experience the author has found that garden books, while seldom lacking in information, often do not present it in the clearest possible way. It has been his aim to make the present volume first of all practical, and in addition to that, though comprehensive, yet simple and concise. If it helps to make the way of the home gardener more clear and definite, its purpose will have been accomplished.

Chapter 1

Introduction

Formerly it was the custom for gardeners to invest their labors and achievements with a mystery and secrecy which might well have discouraged any amateur from trespassing upon such difficult ground. "Trade secrets" in either flower or vegetable growing were acquired by the apprentice only through practice and observation, and in turn jealously guarded by him until passed on to some younger brother in the profession. Every garden operation was made to seem a wonderful and difficult undertaking. Now, all that has changed. In fact the pendulum has swung, as it usually does, to the other extreme. Often, if you are a beginner, you have been flatteringly told in print that you could from the beginning do just as well as the experienced gardener.

My garden friend, it cannot, as a usual thing, be done. Of course, it may happen and sometimes does. You might, being a trusting lamb, go down into Wall Street with $10,000 and make a fortune. You know that you would not be likely to; the chances are very much against you. This garden business is a matter of common sense; and the man, or the woman, who has learned by experience how to do a thing, whether it is cornering the market or growing cabbages, naturally does it better than the one who has not. Do not expect the impossible. If you do, read a poultry advertisement and go into the hen business instead of trying to garden. I have grown pumpkins that necessitated the tearing down of the fence in order to get them out of the lot, and sometimes, though not frequently, have had to use the axe to cut through a stalk of asparagus, but I never "made $17,000 in ten months from an eggplant in a city back-yard." No, if you are going to take up gardening, you will have to work, and you will have a great many disappointments. All that I, or anyone else, could put between the two covers of a book will not make a gardener of you. It must be learned through the fingers, and back, too, as well as from the printed page. But, after all, the greatest reward for your efforts will be the work itself; and unless you love the work, or have a feeling that you will love it, probably the best way for you, is to stick to the grocer for your garden.

Most things, in the course of development, change from the simple to the complex. The art of gardening has in many ways been an exception to the rule. The methods of culture used for many crops are more simple than those in vogue a generation ago. The last fifty years has seen also a tremendous advance in the varieties of vegetables, and the strange thing is that in many instances the new and better sorts are more easily and quickly grown than those they have replaced. The new lima beans are an instance of what is meant. While limas have always been appreciated as one of the most delicious of vegetables, in many sections they could never be successfully grown, because of their aversion to dampness and cold, and of the long season required to mature them. The newer sorts are not only larger and better, but hardier and earlier; and the bush forms have made them still more generally available.

Knowledge on the subject of gardening is also more widely diffused than ever before, and the science of photography has helped wonderfully in telling the newcomer how to do things. It has also lent an impetus and furnished an inspiration which words alone could never have done. If one were to attempt to read all the gardening instructions and suggestions being published, he would have no time left to practice gardening at all. Why then, the reader may ask at this point, another garden book? It is a pertinent question, and it is right that an answer be expected in advance. The reason, then, is this: while there are garden books in plenty, most of them pay more attention to the "content" than to the form in which it is laid before the prospective gardener. The material is often presented as an accumulation of detail, instead of by a systematic and constructive plan which will take the reader step by step through the work to be done, and make clear constantly both the principles and the practice of garden making and management, and at the same time avoid every digression unnecessary from the practical point of view. Other books again, are either so elementary as to be of little use where gardening is done without gloves, or too elaborate, however accurate and worthy in other respects, for an every-day working manual. The author feels, therefore, that there is a distinct field for the present book.

And, while I still have the reader by the "introduction" buttonhole, I want to make a suggestion or two about using a book like this. Do not, on the one hand, read it through and then put it away with the dictionary and the family Bible, and trust to memory for the instruction it may give; do not, on the other hand, wait until you think it is time to plant a thing, and then go and look it up. For instance, do not, about the middle of May, begin investigating how many onion seeds to put in a hill; you will find out that they should have been put in, in drills, six weeks before. Read the whole book through carefully at your first opportunity, make a list of the things you should do for your own vegetable garden, and put opposite them the proper dates for your own vicinity. Keep this available, as a working guide, and refer to special matters as you get to them.

Do not feel discouraged that you cannot be promised immediate success at the start. I know from personal experience and from the experience of others that "book-gardening" is a practical thing. If you do your work carefully and thoroughly, you may be confident that a very great measure of success will reward the efforts of your first garden season.

And I know too, that you will find it the most entrancing game you ever played.

Good luck to you!

Chapter 2

Why You Should Garden

There are more reasons to-day than ever before why the owner of a small place should have his, or her, own vegetable garden. The days of home weaving, home cheese-making, home meat-packing, are gone. With a thousand and one other things that used to be made or done at home, they have left the fireside and followed the factory chimney. These things could be turned over to machinery. The growing of vegetables cannot be so disposed of. Garden tools have been improved, but they are still the same old one-man affairs—doing one thing, one row at a time. Labor is still the big factor—and that, taken in combination with the cost of transporting and handling such perishable stuff as garden produce, explains why the home gardener can grow his own vegetables at less expense than he can buy them. That is a good fact to remember.

But after all, I doubt if most of us will look at the matter only after consulting the columns of the household ledger. The big thing, the salient feature of home gardening is not that we may get our vegetables ten per cent. cheaper, but that we can have them one hundred per cent. better. Even the long-keeping sorts, like squash, potatoes and onions, are very perceptibly more delicious right from the home garden, fresh from the vines or the ground; but when it comes to peas, and corn, and lettuce,—well, there is absolutely nothing to compare with the home garden ones, gathered fresh, in the early slanting sunlight, still gemmed with dew, still crisp and tender and juicy, ready to carry every atom of savory quality, without loss, to the dining table. Stale, flat and unprofitable indeed, after these have once been tasted, seem the limp, travel-weary, dusty things that are jounced around to us in the butcher's cart and the grocery wagon. It is not in price alone that home gardening pays. There is another point: the market gardener has to grow the things that give the biggest yield. He has to sacrifice quality to quantity. You do not. One cannot buy Golden Bantam corn, or Mignonette lettuce, or Gradus peas in most markets. They are top quality, but they do not fill the market crate enough times to the row to pay the commercial grower. If you cannot afford to keep a professional gardener there is only one way to have the best vegetables—grow your own!

And this brings us to the third, and what may be the most important reason why you should garden. It is the cheapest, healthiest, keenest pleasure there is. Give me a sunny garden patch in the golden springtime, when the trees are picking out their new gowns, in all the various self-colored delicate grays and greens—strange how beautiful they are, in the same old unchanging styles, isn't it?—give me seeds to watch as they find the light, plants to tend as they take hold in the fine, loose, rich soil, and you may have the other sports. And when you have grown tired of their monotony, come back in summer to even the smallest garden, and you will find in it, every day, a new problem to be solved, a new campaign to be carried out, a new victory to win.

Better food, better health, better living—all these the home garden offers you in abundance. And the price is only the price of every worthwhile thing—honest, cheerful patient work.

But enough for now of the dream garden. Put down your book. Put on your old togs, light your pipe—some kind-hearted humanitarian should devise for women such a kindly and comforting vice as smoking—and let's go outdoors and look the place over, and pick out the best spot for that garden-patch of yours.

Chapter 3

Requisites of the Home Vegetable Garden

In deciding upon the site for the home vegetable garden it is well to dispose once and for all of the old idea that the garden "patch" must be an ugly spot in the home surroundings. If thoughtfully planned, carefully planted and thoroughly cared for, it may be made a beautiful and harmonious feature of the general scheme, lending a touch of comfortable homeliness that no shrubs, borders, or beds can ever produce.

With this fact in mind we will not feel restricted to any part of the premises merely because it is out of sight behind the barn or garage. In the average moderate-sized place there will not be much choice as to land. It will be necessary to take what is to be had and then do the very best that can be done with it. But there will probably be a good deal of choice as to, first, exposure, and second, convenience. Other things being equal, select a spot near at hand, easy of access. It may seem that a difference of only a few hundred yards will mean nothing, but if one is depending largely upon spare moments for working in and for watching the garden—and in the growing of many vegetables the latter is almost as important as the former—this matter of convenient access will be of much greater importance than is likely to be at first recognized. Not until you have had to make a dozen time-wasting trips for forgotten seeds or tools, or gotten your feet soaking wet by going out through the dew-drenched grass, will you realize fully what this may mean.

EXPOSURE

But the thing of first importance to consider in picking out the spot that is to yield you happiness and delicious vegetables all summer, or even for many years, is the exposure. Pick out the "earliest" spot you can find—a plot sloping a little to the south or east, that seems to catch sunshine early and hold it late, and that seems to be out of the direct path of the chilling north and northeast winds. If a building, or even an old fence, protects it from this direction, your garden will be helped along wonderfully, for an early start is a great big factor toward success. If it is not already protected, a board fence, or a hedge of some low-growing shrubs or young evergreens, will add very greatly to its usefulness. The importance of having such a protection or shelter is altogether underestimated by the amateur.

THE SOIL

The chances are that you will not find a spot of ideal garden soil ready for use anywhere upon your place. But all except the very worst of soils can be brought up to a very high degree of productiveness— especially such small areas as home vegetable gardens require. Large tracts of soil that are almost pure sand, and others so heavy and mucky that for centuries they lay uncultivated, have frequently been brought, in the course of only a few years, to where they yield annually tremendous crops on a commercial basis. So do not be discouraged about your soil. Proper treatment of it is much more important, and a garden- patch of average run-down,—or "never-brought-up" soil—will produce much more for the energetic and careful gardener than the richest spot will grow under average methods of cultivation.

The ideal garden soil is a "rich, sandy loam." And the fact cannot be overemphasized that such soils usually are made, not found. Let us analyze that description a bit, for right here we come to the first of the four all-important factors of gardening—food. The others are cultivation, moisture and temperature. "Rich" in the gardener's vocabulary means full of plant food; more than that—and this is a point of vital importance—it means full of plant food ready to be used at once, all prepared and spread out on the garden table, or rather in it, where growing things can at once make use of it; or what we term, in one word, "available" plant food. Practically no soils in long- inhabited communities remain naturally rich enough to produce big crops. They are made rich, or kept rich, in two ways; first, by cultivation, which helps to change the raw plant food stored in the soil into available forms; and second, by manuring or adding plant food to the soil from outside sources.

"Sandy" in the sense here used, means a soil containing enough particles of sand so that water will pass through it without leaving it pasty and sticky a few days after a rain; "light" enough, as it is called, so that a handful, under ordinary conditions, will crumble and fall apart readily after being pressed in the hand. It is not necessary that the soil be sandy in appearance, but it should be friable.

"Loam: a rich, friable soil," says Webster. That hardly covers it, but it does describe it. It is soil in which the sand and clay are in proper proportions, so that neither greatly predominate, and usually dark in color, from cultivation and enrichment. Such a soil, even to the untrained eye, just naturally looks as if it would grow things. It is remarkable how quickly the whole physical appearance of a piece of well cultivated ground will change. An instance came under my notice last fall in one of my fields, where a strip containing an acre had been two years in onions, and a little piece jutting off from the middle of this had been prepared for them just one season. The rest had not received any extra manuring or cultivation. When the field was plowed up in the fall, all three sections were as distinctly noticeable as though separated by a fence. And I know that next spring's crop of rye, before it is plowed under, will show the lines of demarcation just as plainly.

This, then, will give you an idea of a good garden soil. Perhaps in yours there will be too much sand, or too much clay. That will be a disadvantage, but one which energy and perseverance will soon overcome to a great extent—by what methods may be learned in Chapter VIII.

DRAINAGE

There is, however, one other thing you must look out for in selecting your garden site, and that is drainage. Dig down eight or twelve inches after you have picked out a favorable spot, and examine the subsoil. This is the second strata, usually of different texture and color from the rich surface soil, and harder than it. If you find a sandy or gravelly bed, no matter how yellow and poor it looks, you have chosen the right spot. But if it be a stiff, heavy clay, especially a blue clay, you will have either to drain it or be content with a very late garden—that is, unless you are at the top of a knoll or on a slope. Chapter VII contains further suggestions in regard to this problem.

SOIL ANTECEDENTS

There was a further reason for, mentioning that strip of onion ground. It is a very practical illustration of what last year's handling of the soil means to this year's garden. If you can pick out a spot, even if it is not the most desirable in other ways, that has been well enriched or cultivated for a year or two previous, take that for this year's garden. And in the meantime have the spot on which you intend to make your permanent vegetable garden thoroughly "fitted," and grow there this year a crop of potatoes or sweet corn, as suggested in Chapter IX. Then next year you will have conditions just right to give your vegetables a great start.

OTHER CONSIDERATIONS

There are other things of minor importance but worth considering, such as the shape of your garden plot, for instance. The more nearly rectangular, the more convenient it will be to work and the more easily kept clean and neat. Have it large enough, or at least open on two ends, so that a horse can be used in plowing and harrowing. And if by any means you can have it within reach of an adequate supply of water, that will be a tremendous help in seasons of protracted drought. Then again, if you have ground enough, lay off two plots so that you can take advantage of the practice of rotation, alternating grass, potatoes or corn with the vegetable garden. Of course it is possible to practice crop rotation to some extent within the limits of even the small vegetable garden, but it will be much better, if possible, to rotate the entire garden-patch.

All these things, then, one has to keep in mind in picking the spot best suited for the home vegetable garden. It should be, if possible, of convenient access; it should have a warm exposure and be well enriched, well worked-up soil, not too light nor too heavy, and by all means well drained. If it has been thoroughly cultivated for a year or two previous, so much the better. If it is near a supply of water, so situated that it can be at least plowed and harrowed with a horse, and large enough to allow the garden proper to be shifted every other year or two, still more the better.

Fill all of these requirements that you can, and then by taking full advantage of the advantages you have, you can discount the disadvantages. After all it is careful, persistent work, more than natural advantages, that will tell the story; and a good garden does not grow—it is made.

Chapter 4

The Planting Plan

Having selected the garden spot, the next consideration, naturally, is what shall be planted in it.

The old way was to get a few seed catalogues, pick out a list of the vegetables most enthusiastically described by the (wholly disinterested) seedsman, and then, when the time came, to put them in at one or two plantings, and sowing each kind as far as the seed would go. There is a better way—a way to make the garden produce more, to yield things when you want them, and in the proper proportions.

All these advantages, you may suppose, must mean more work. On the contrary, however, the new way makes very much less work and makes results a hundred per cent. more certain. It is not necessary even that more thought be put upon the garden, but forethought there must be. Forethought, however, is much more satisfactory than hindthought.

In the new way of gardening there are four great helps, four things that will be of great assistance to the experienced gardener, and that are indispensable to the success of the beginner. They are the Planting Plan, the Planting Table, the Check List and the Garden Record.

Do not become discouraged at the formidable sound of that paragraph and decide that after all you do not want to fuss so much over your garden; that you are doing it for the fun of the thing anyway, and such intricate systems will not be worth bothering with. The purpose of those four garden helps is simply to make your work less and your returns more. You might just as well refuse to use a wheel hoe because the trowel was good enough for your grandmother's garden, as to refuse to take advantage of the modern garden methods described in this chapter. Without using them to some extent, or in some modified form, you can never know just what you are doing with your garden or what improvements to make next year. Of course, each of the plans or lists suggested here is only one of many possible combinations. You should be able to find, or better still to construct, similar ones better suited to your individual taste, need and opportunity. That, however, does not lessen the necessity of using some such system. It is just as necessary an aid to the maximum efficiency in gardening as are modern tools. Do not fear that you will waste time on the planting plan. Master it and use it, for only so can you make your garden time count for most in producing results.

In the average small garden there is a very large percentage of waste—for two weeks, more string beans than can be eaten or given away; and then, for a month, none at all, for instance. You should determine ahead as nearly as possible how much of each vegetable your table will require and then try to grow enough of each for a continuous supply, and no more. It is just this that the planting plan enables you to do.

I shall describe, as briefly as possible, forms of the planting plan, planting table, check list and record, which I have found it convenient to use.

To make the Planting Plan take a sheet of white paper and a ruler and mark off a space the shape of your garden—which should be rectangular if possible—using a scale of one-quarter or one-eighth inch to the foot. Rows fifty feet long will be found a convenient length for the average home garden. In a garden where many varieties of things are grown it will be best to run the rows the short way of the piece. We will take a fifty-foot row for the purpose of illustration, though of course it can readily be changed in proportion where rows of that length cannot conveniently be made. In a very small garden it will be better to make the row, say, twenty-five feet long, the aim being always to keep the row a unit and have as few broken ones as possible, and still not to have to plant more of any one thing than will be needed.

In assigning space for the various vegetables several things should be kept in mind in order to facilitate planting, replanting and cultivating the garden. These can most quickly be realized by a glance at the plan illustrated herewith. You will notice that crops that remain several years—rhubarb and asparagus—are kept at one end. Next come such as will remain a whole season—parsnips, carrots, onions and the like. And finally those that will be used for a succession of crops—peas, lettuce, spinach. Moreover, tall-growing crops, like pole beans, are kept to the north of lower ones. In the plan illustrated the space given to each variety is allotted according to the proportion in which they are ordinarily used. If it happens that you have a special weakness for peas, or your mother-in-law an aversion to peppers, keep these tastes and similar ones in mind when laying out your planting plan.

Do not leave the planning of your garden until you are ready to put the seeds in the ground and then do it all in a rush. Do it in January, as soon as you have received the new year's catalogues and when you have time to study over them and look up your record of the previous year. Every hour spent on the plan will mean several hours saved in the garden.

The Planting Table is the next important system in the business of gardening, especially for the beginner. In it one can see at a glance all the details of the particular treatment each vegetable requires— when to sow, how deep, how far apart the rows should be, etc. I remember how many trips from garden to house to hunt through catalogues for just such information I made in my first two seasons' gardening. How much time, just at the very busiest season of the whole year, such a table would have saved!

Where can you *buy* vegetables like these, gathered fresh in the morning, sparkling with crystal dew?

Even the smallest country place should have a greenhouse. It is surprising how satisfactorily one can be built at a low cost by buying the materials and doing the work yourself

The Planting Table prepared for one's own use should show, besides the information given, the varieties of each vegetable which experience has proved best adapted to one's own needs. The table shown herewith gives such a list; varieties which are for the most part standard favorites and all of which, with me, have proven reliable, productive and of good quality. Other good sorts will be found described in Part Two. Such a table should be mounted on cardboard and kept where it may readily be referred to at planting time.

The Check List is the counterpart of the planting table, so arranged that its use will prevent anything from being overlooked or left until too late. Prepare it ahead, sometime in January, when you have time to think of everything. Make it up from your planting table and from the previous year's record. From this list it will be well to put down on a sheet of paper the things to be done each month (or week) and cross them off as they are attended to. Without some such system it is almost a certainty that you will overlook some important things.

The Garden Record is no less important. It may be kept in the simplest sort of way, but be sure to keep it. A large piece of paper ruled as follows, for instance, will require only a few minutes' attention each week and yet will prove of the greatest assistance in planning the garden next season.

The Vegetable Garden Record shows how such a record will be kept. Of course, only the first column is written in ahead. I want to emphasize in passing, however, the importance of putting down your data on the day you plant, or harvest, or notice anything worth recording. If you let it go until tomorrow it is very apt to be lacking next year.

Try these four short-cuts to success, even if you have had a garden before. They will make a big difference in your garden; less work and greater results.

```
  0   5  10  15  20  25  30  35  40  45  50
 ┌──────────────────────────────────────────┐
 │         RHUBARB-2       │P│R│  SEED-BED  │
 ├──────────────────────────────────────────┤
 │              ASPARAGUS-2                 │
 ├──────────────────────────────────────────┤
 │              POLE BEANS-2                │
 ├──────────────────────────────────────────┤
 │              TOMATOES-1                  │
 ├──────────────────────────────────────────┤
 │       CABBAGE  EARLY-1                   │
 │                LATE-1                    │
 ├──────────────────────────────────────────┤
 │         CAULIFLOWER, EARLY-1             │
 ├───────────────────┬──────────────────────┤
 │   BROCOLLI-1      │  BRUSSELS SPROUTS-1  │
 ├───────────────────┼──────────────────────┤
 │   PEPPERS-1       │     EGG-PLANT-1      │
 ├──────────────────────────────────────────┤
 │              CELERY-1                    │
 ├──────────────────────────────────────────┤
 │              ONIONS-3½                   │
 │              LEEKS-½                     │
 ├──────────────────────────────────────────┤
 │              CARROTS-4                   │
 ├──────────────────────────────────────────┤
 │              BEETS-4                     │
 ├───────────────────┬──────────────────────┤
 │   TURNIPS-1½      │    RUTABAGA-½        │
 ├──────────────────────────────────────────┤
 │              PARSNIPS-1                  │
 ├──────────────────────────────────────────┤
 │                                          │
 │              CORN-4                      │
 │                                          │
 ├──────────────────────────────────────────┤
 │                                          │
 │              PEAS-3                      │
 │                                          │
 ├──────────────────────────────────────────┤
 │              BUSH BEANS-3                │
 ├──────────────────────────────────────────┤
 │              LETTUCE-2                   │
 ├───────────────────┬──────────────────────┤
 │   ONION SETS-1    │      ENDIVE-1        │
 ├───────────────────┼──────────────────────┤
 │  MUSKMELONS-6Hills│  CUCUMBERS-7Hills    │
 ├───────────────────┼──────────────────────┤
 │  PUMPKINS-4H.     │  WATERMELONS-5H.     │
 ├───────────────────┼──────────────────────┤
 │                   │ SUMMER SQUASH,BUSH-5H│
 │  WINTER SQUASH-5H.├──────────────────────┤
 │                   │ SUMMER SQUASH,VINE-5H│
 └───────────────────┴──────────────────────┘
```

A typical Planting Plan. The scale measurements at the left and top indicate the length and distance apart of rows.

PLANTING TABLE

VEGETABLE	PLANT[1]	DEPTH TO SOW—INS.	DISTANCE APART	
			SEEDS[2]	ROWS
I. CROPS REMAINING ENTIRE SEASON				
Asparagus, seed	April-May	1	2-4 in.	15 in.
Asparagus, plants	April	4	1 ft.	3 ft.
Bean, pole	May 15-June 10	2	3 ft.	3 ft.
Bean, lima	May 20-June 10	2	3 ft.	3 ft.
Beet, late	April-August	2	3-4 in.	15 in.
Carrot, late	May-July	½-1	2-3 in.	15 in.
Corn, late	May 20-July 10	2	3 ft.	4 ft.
Cucumber	May 10-July 15	1	4 ft.	4 ft.
Egg-plant, plants	June 1-20	..	2 ft.	30 in.
Leek	April	..	2-4 in	15 in.
Melon, musk	May 15-June 15	1	4 ft.	4 ft.
Melon, water	May 15-June 15	1	6-8 ft.	6-8 ft.
Onion	April	½-1	2-4 in.	15 in.
Okra	May 15-June 15	½-1	2 ft.	3 ft.
Parsley[4]	April-May	½	4-6 in.	1 ft.
Parsnip	April	½-1	3-5 in.	18 in.
Pepper, seed	June 1st	½	3-6 in.	15 in.
Pepper, plants	June 1-20	..	2 ft.	30 in.
Potatoes, main	April 15-June 20	4-6	13 in.	30 in.
Pumpkins	May 1-June 20	1-2	6-8 ft.	6-8 ft.
Rhubarb, plants	April	..	2-3 ft.	3 ft.
Salsify	April-May	1	3-6 in.	18 in.
Squash, summer	May 15-July 1	1-2	4 ft.	4 ft.
Squash, winter	May 15-June 20	1-2	6-8 ft.	6-8 ft.
Tomato, seed	June	½	3-4 in.	15 in.
Tomato, plants	May 15-July 20	..	3 ft.	3 ft.

Home Vegetable Gardening

VEGETABLE	SEED FOR 50 FT. ROW	VARIETIES
Asparagus, seed...	1 oz.	Palmetto, Giant Argenteuil, Barr's Mammoth
Asparagus, plants.	50	Palmetto, Giant Argenteuil, Barr's Mammoth
Bean pole........	½ pt.	Kentucky Wonder, Golden, Cluster, Burger's Stringless
Bean, lima,......	½ pt.	Early Leviathan, Giant Podded, Burpee Improved
Beet, late.......	1 oz.	Crimson Globe
Carrot, late......	½ oz.	Danver's Half-long, Ox-heart, Chantenay
Corn, late,.......	½ pt.	Seymour's Sweet Orange, White Evergreen, Country Gentleman
Cucumber........	½ oz.	Early White Spine, Fordhook Famous, Davis Perfect
Egg-plant, plants.	25	Black Beauty, N. Y. Purple
Leek............	½ oz.	American Flag
Melon, musk.....	½ oz.	Netted Gem, Emerald Gem, Hoodoo
Melon, water.....	¼ oz.	Cole's Early, Sweetheart, Halbert Honey
Onion...........	½ oz.	Prizetaker, Danver's Globe, Ailsa Craig, Southport Red Globe, Mammoth Silverskin (white)
Okra............	½ oz.	Perfected Perkins, White Velvet
Parsley..........	½ oz.	Emerald
Parsnip..........	¼ oz.	Hollow Crowned (Improved)
Pepper, seed.....	½ oz.	Ruby King, Chinese Giant
Pepper, plants.....	25	Ruby King, Chinese Giant
Potatoes, main....	½ pk.	Irish Cobbler, Green Mountain, Uncle Sam (Noroton Beauty, Norwood, early)
Pumpkins........	¼ oz.	Large Cheese, Quaker Pie
Rhubarb, plants..	25	Myatt's Victoria
Salsify..........	1 oz.	Mammoth Sandwich
Squash, summer...	¼ oz.	White Bush, Delicata, Fordhook, Vegetable Marrow
Squash, winter....	¼ oz.	Hubbard, Delicious
Tomato, seed.....	½ oz.	Earliana, Chalk's Jewel, Matchless, Dwarf Giant
Tomato, plants....	20	Earliana, Chalk's Jewel, Matchless, Dwarf Giant

PLAN

VEGETABLE	PLANT[1]	DEPTH TO SOW—INS.	DISTANCE APART	
			SEEDS[3]	ROWS
II. CROPS FOR SUCCESSION PLANTINGS				
Bean, dwarf......	May 5-Aug. 15....	2	2-4 in.	1½-2 ft.
Kohlrabi[4]........	April-July........	½-1	6-12 in.	1½-2 ft.
Lettuce[4].........	April-August.....	½	1 ft.	1-1½ ft.
Peas, smooth.....	April 1-Aug. 1...	2-3	2-4 in.	3 ft.
Peas, wrinkled....	April 10-July 15..	2-3	2-4 in.	3-4 ft.
Radish...........	April 1-Sept 1....	½	2-3 in.	1 ft.
Spinach..........	April-Sept 15.....	1	3-5 in.	18 in.
Turnip...........	April-Sept.......	½-1	4-6 in.	15 in.
III. CROPS TO BE FOLLOWED BY OTHERS				
Beet, early.......	April-June.......	2	3-4 in.	15 in.
Broccoli, early[4]...	April............	½-1	1½ ft.	2 ft.
Borecole[4]........	April............	½-1	2 ft.	2½ ft.
Brussels sprouts[4]...	April............	½-1	1½ ft.	2 ft.
Cabbage, early[4]....	April............	½-1	1½ ft.	2 ft.
Carrot...........	April............	½-1	2-3 in.	15 in.
Cauliflower[4]......	April............	½-1	1½ ft.	2 ft.
Corn, early.......	May 10-20.......	2	3 ft.	3-4 ft.
Onion sets........	April-May 15.....	1-2	2-4 in.	15 in.
Peas.............	April 1-May 1....	2	2-4 in.	3 ft.
Crops in Sec. II.				
IV. CROPS THAT MAY FOLLOW OTHERS				
Beet, late........	July-August......	2	3-4 in.	15 in
Borecole..........	May-June[2].......	½-1	2 ft.	2½ ft.
Broccoli..........	May-June[2].......	½-1	2 ft.	2½ ft.
Brussels sprouts...	May-June[2].......	½-1	1½ ft.	2½ ft.
Cabbage late.....	May-June[2].......	½-1	2½ ft.	2½ ft.
Cauliflower.......	May-June[2].......	½-1	2 ft.	2½ ft.
Celery, seed......	April............	½	1-2 in.	1 ft.
Celery, plant.....	July 1-Aug. 1.....	..	6 in.	3-4 ft.
Endive[4]..........	April-August.....	½	1 ft.	1 ft.
Peas, late........	May 15-Aug. 1...	2-3	2-4 in.	4 ft.
Crops in Sec. II.				

28 HOME VEGETABLE GARDENING

VEGETABLE	SEED FOR 50 FT. ROW	VARIETIES
II. CROPS FOR SUCCESSION PLANTINGS		
Bean, dwarf.....	1 pt.	Red Valentine, Burpee's Greenpod, Improved Refugee, Brittle Wax, Rust-proof Golden Wax, Burpee's White Wax
Kohlrabi........	¼ oz.	White Vienna
Lettuce.........	50	Mignonette, Grand Rapids, May King, Big Boston, New York, Deacon, Cos, Paris White
Peas, smooth.....	1 pt.	American Wonder
Peas, wrinkled...	1 pt.	Gradus, Boston Unrivaled, Quite Content
Radish..........	½ oz.	Rapid Red, Crimson Globe, Chinese
Spinach.........	½ oz.	Swiss Chard Beet, Long Season, Victoria
Turnip..........	½ oz.	White Milan, Petrowski, Golden Ball
III. CROPS TO BE FOLLOWED BY OTHERS		
Beet, early......	1 oz.	Edmund's Early, Early Model
Broccoli, early...	35	Early White French
Borecole........	25	Dwarf Scotch Curled
Brussels sprouts..	35	Dalkeith, Danish Prize
Cabbage, early...	35	Wakefield, Glory of Enkhuisen, Early Summer, Succession, Savoy
Carrot..........	½ oz.	Golden Ball, Early Scarlet Horn
Cauliflower......	35	Burpee's Best Early, Snowball, Sea-foam Dry Weather
Corn, early......	½ pt.	Golden Bantam, Peep o' Day, Cory
Onion sets.......	2 pt.	
Peas............	1 pt.	
Crops in Sec. II.		
IV. CROPS THAT MAY FOLLOW OTHERS		
Beet, late.......	1 oz.	Crimson Globe
Borecole........	25	Dwarf Scotch Curled
Broccoli.........	25	Early White French
Brussels sprouts..	35	Dalkeith, Danish Prize
Cabbage, late....	25	Succession, Danish Ballhead Drumhead
Cauliflower......	25	As above. [Savoy, Mammoth Rock (red)
Celery, seed.....	1 oz.	White Plume, Golden Self-blanching, Winter Queen
Celery, plant....	100	White Plume, Golden Self-blanching, Winter Queen
Endive..........	½ oz.	Broad-Leaved Batavian, Giant Fringed
Peas, late.......	1 pt.	Gradus
Crops in Sec. II.		

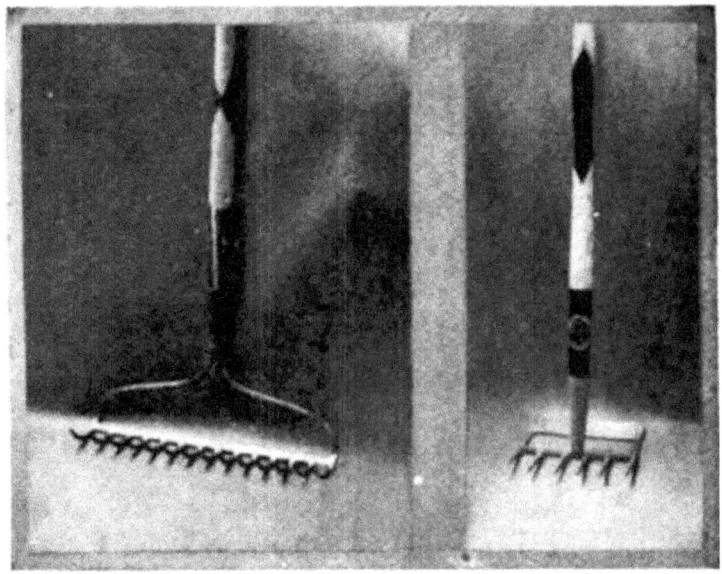

Select a bow-head rake rather than one in which the teeth-bar is fastened directly to the shaft. At the right is the useful prong-hoe

Four types of hoe; from the left, the scuffle-hoe, the heart-shaped hoe, the short hoe, and the common hoe

F. F. ROCKWELL

If you have a wheel hoe with the drill seeder attachment, the whole process of planting can be simplified. The cost is $11 for both

The labor of both hoeing and hand-weeding will be reduced to a minimum if you will spend a few dollars for a wheel hoe

VEGETABLE GARDEN RECORD—1910

Vegetable	Variety	Put in	Ready	Notes
Beans, dwarf	Red Valentine...	May 10	July 6	Not best quality. Try other earlies
	Golden Wax....	May 15	July 22	Rusted. Spray next year
Bean, pole..	Old Homestead..	May 16	July 26	Too many. 6 poles next year
	Early Leviathan	May 25	Aug. 19	Good. Dry.
Bean, lima..	Fordhook......	May 15	....	Rotted. Try May 25
Beet	Egyptian	Apr. 10	June 12	Roots sprangled
	Eclipse.........	Apr. 10	June 14	Better quality
Cabbage....	Wakefield......	Apr. 9	June 20	Injured by worms. Hellebore next year
Etc., etc.				

CHECK LIST

Jan. 1st—Send for catalogues. Make planting plan and table. Order seeds.

Feb. 1st—Inside: cabbage, cauliflower, first sowing. Onions for plants.

Feb. 15th—Inside: lettuce, cabbage, cauliflower, Brussels sprouts, beets.

March 1st—Inside: lettuce, celery, tomato (early).

March 15th—Inside: lettuce, tomato (main), eggplant, pepper, lima beans, cucumber, squash; sprout potatoes in sand.

April 1st—Inside: cauliflower (on sods), muskmelon, watermelon, corn. Outside: (seed-bed) celery, cabbage, lettuce. Onions, carrots, smooth peas, spinach, beets, chard, parsnip, turnip, radish. Lettuce, cabbage (plants).

May 1st—Beans, corn, spinach, lettuce, radish.

May 15th—Beans, limas, muskmelon, watermelon, summer squash, peas, potatoes, lettuce, radish, tomato (early), corn, limas, melon, cucumber and squash (plants). Pole-lima, beets, corn, kale, winter squash, pumpkin, lettuce, radish.

June 1st—Beans, carrots, corn, cucumber, peas, summer spinach, summer lettuce, radish, egg-plant, pepper, tomato (main plants).

June 15th—Beans, corn, peas, turnip, summer lettuce, radish, late cabbage, and tomato plants.

July 1st—Beans, endive, kale, lettuce, radish, winter cabbage, cauliflower, Brussels sprouts and celery plants.

July 15th—Beans, early corn, early peas, lettuce, radish.

Aug. 1st—Early peas, lettuce, radish.

Aug. 15th—Early peas, lettuce, radish in seed-bed, forcing lettuce for fall in frames.

Sept. 1st—Lettuce, radish, spinach and onions for wintering over.

F. F. ROCKWELL

NOTE.—This list is for planting only (the dates are approximate: see note I at the end of the chapter). Spraying and other garden operations may also be included in such a list. See "Calendar of Operations" at end of book.

Chapter 5

Implements and Their Uses

It may seem to the reader that it is all very well to make a garden with a pencil, but that the work of transferring it to the soil must be quite another problem and one entailing so much work that he will leave it to the professional market gardener. He possibly pictures to himself some bent-kneed and stoop-shouldered man with the hoe, and decides that after all there is too much work in the garden game. What a revelation would be in store for him if he could witness one day's operations in a modern market garden! Very likely indeed not a hoe would be seen during the entire visit. Modern implements, within less than a generation, have revolutionized gardening.

This is true of the small garden as certainly as of the large one: in fact, in proportion I am not sure but that it is more so—because of the second wonderful thing about modern garden tools, that is, the low prices at which they can be bought, considering the enormous percentage of labor saved in accomplishing results. There is nothing in the way of expense to prevent even the most modest gardener acquiring, during a few years, by the judicious expenditure of but a few dollars annually, a very complete outfit of tools that will handsomely repay their cost.

While some garden tools have been improved and developed out of all resemblance to their original forms, others have changed little in generations, and in probability will remain ever with us. There is a thing or two to say about even the simplest of them, however,— especially to anyone not familiar with their uses.

There are tools for use in every phase of horticultural operations; for preparing the ground, for planting the seed, for cultivation, for protecting crops from insects and disease, and for harvesting.

First of all comes the ancient and honorable spade, which, for small garden plots, borders, beds, etc., must still be relied upon for the initial operation in gardening—breaking up the soil. There are several types, but any will answer the purpose. In buying a spade look out for two things: see that it is well strapped up the handle in front and back, and that it hangs well. In spading up ground, especially soil that is turfy or hard, the work may be made easier by taking a strip not quite twice as wide as the spade, and making diagonal cuts so that one vertical edge of the spade at each thrust cuts clean out to where the soil has already been dug. The wide-tined spading-fork is frequently used instead of the spade, as it is lighter and can be more advantageously used to break up lumps and level off surfaces. In most soils it will do this work as well, if not better, than the spade and has the further good quality of being serviceable as a fork too, thus combining two tools in one. It should be more generally known and used. With the ordinary fork, used for handling manure and gathering up trash, weeds, etc., every gardener is familiar. The type with oval, slightly up-curved tines, five or six in number, and a D handle, is the most convenient and comfortable for garden use.

For areas large enough for a horse to turn around in, use a plow. There are many good makes. The swivel type has the advantage of turning all the furrows one way, and is the best for small plots and sloping ground. It should turn a clean, deep furrow. In deep soil that has long been cultivated, plowing should, with few exceptions, be down at least to the subsoil; and if the soil is shallow it will be advisable to turn up a little of the subsoil, at each plowing—not more than an inch—in order that the soil may gradually be deepened. In plowing sod it will be well to have the plow fitted with a coulter, which turns a miniature furrow ahead of the plowshare, thus covering under all sods and grass and getting them out of the way of harrows and other tools to be used later. In plowing under tall-growing green manures, like rye, a heavy chain is hung from the evener to the handle, thus pulling the crop down into the furrow so that it will all be covered under. Where drainage is poor it will be well to break up the subsoil with a subsoil plow, which follows in the wake of the regular plow but does not lift the subsoil to the surface.

TOOLS FOR PREPARING THE SEED-BED

The spade or spading-fork will be followed by the hoe, or hook, and the iron rake; and the plow by one or more of the various types of harrow. The best type of hoe for use after the spade is the wide, deep-bladed type. In most soils, however, this work may be done more expeditiously with the hook or prong-hoe (see illustration). With this the soil can be thoroughly pulverized to a depth of several inches. In using either, be careful not to pull up manure or trash turned under by the spade, as all such material if left covered will quickly rot away in the soil and furnish the best sort of plant food. I should think that our energetic manufactures would make a prong-hoe with heavy wide blades, like those of the spading-fork, but I have never seen such an implement, either in use or advertised.

What the prong-hoe is to the spade, the harrow is to the plow. For general purposes the Acme is an excellent harrow. It is adjustable, and for ground at all mellow will be the only one necessary; set it, for the first time over, to cut in deep; and then, set for leveling, it will leave the soil in such excellent condition that a light hand- raking (or, for large areas, the Meeker smoothing-harrow) will prepare it for the finest of seeds, such as onions and carrots. The teeth of the Acme are so designed that they practically constitute a gang of miniature plows. Of disc harrows there are a great many makes. The salient feature of the disc type is that they can tear up no manure, grass or trash, even when these are but partly turned under by the plow. For this reason it is especially useful on sod or other rough ground. The most convenient harrow for putting on the finishing touches, for leveling off and fining the surface of the soil, is the lever spike-tooth. It is adjustable and can be used as a spike-tooth or as a smoothing harrow.

 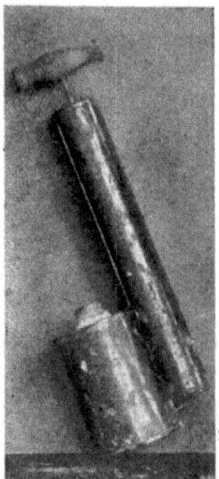

There are many types of hand "dusters" and sprayers, one at least of which will be necessary in the home garden. Of the sprayers always buy brass implements

Any of the harrows mentioned above (except the Meeker) and likewise the prong-hoe, will have to be followed by the iron rake when preparing the ground for small-seeded garden vegetables. Get the sort with what is termed the "bow" head (see illustration) instead of one in which the head is fastened directly to the end of the handle. It is less likely to get broken, and easier to use. There is quite a knack in manipulating even a garden rake, which will come only with practice. Do not rake as though you were gathering up leaves or grass. The secret in using the garden rake is not to gather things up. Small stones, lumps of earth and such things, you of course wish to remove. Keep these raked off ahead of where you are leveling the soil, which is accomplished with a backward-and-forward movement of the rake.

The tool-house of every garden of any size should contain a seed-drill. Labor which is otherwise tedious and difficult is by it rendered mere play—as well as being better done.

A barrel-pump suitable for spraying on a larger scale—useful in the home orchard

The operations of marking the row, opening the furrow, dropping the seed at the proper depth and distance, covering immediately with fresh earth, and firming the soil, are all done at one fell swoop and as fast as you can walk. It will even drop seeds in hills. But that is not all: it may be had as part of a combination machine, which, after your seeds are planted—with each row neatly rolled on top, and plainly visible—may be at once transformed into a wheel hoe that will save you as much time in caring for your plants as the seed-drill did in planting your seed. Hoeing drudgery becomes a thing of the past. The illustration herewith shows such a machine, and some of the varied attachments which may be had for it. There are so many, and so varied in usefulness, that it would require an entire chapter to detail their special advantages and methods of use. The catalogues describing them will give you many valuable suggestions; and other ways of utilizing them will discover themselves to you in your work.

A fine way to manage the compost heap—no waste and no unsightly pile

Valuable as the wheel hoe is, however, and varied in its scope of work, the time-tried hoe cannot be entirely dispensed with. An accompanying photograph shows four distinct types, all of which will pay for themselves in a garden of moderate size.

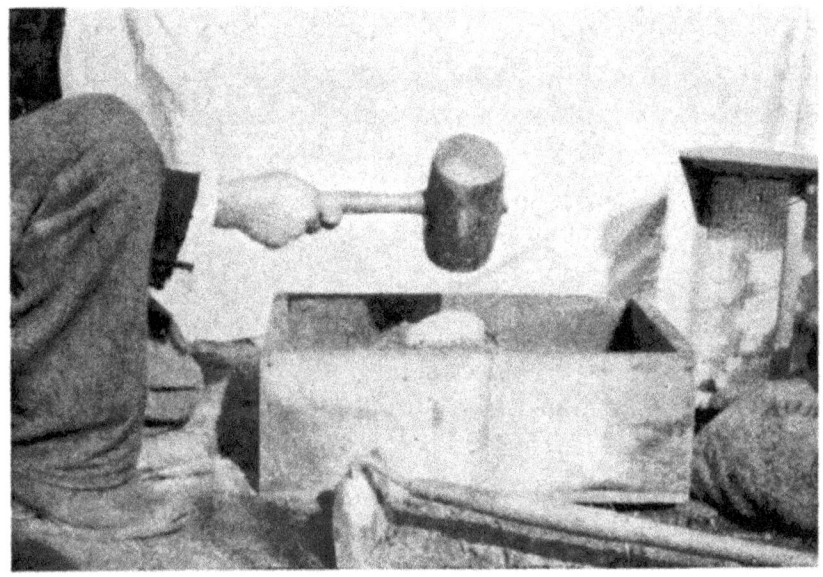

In order to be able to supply your garden soil with the elements of plant food it really needs, you will have to keep a record of production under various conditions, and then mix your fertilizers in the proper proportions to suit. Break up all lumps and mix the ingredients by hoeing in a box

The one on the right is the one most generally seen; next to it is a modified form which personally I prefer for all light work, such as loosening soil and cutting out weeds. It is lighter and smaller, quicker and easier to handle. Next to this is the Warren, or heart-shaped hoe, especially valuable in opening and covering drills for seed, such as beans, peas or corn. The scuffle-hoe, or scarifier, which completes the four, is used between narrow rows for shallow work, such as cutting off small weeds and breaking up the crust. It has been rendered less frequently needed by the advent of the wheel hoe, but when crops are too large to admit of the use of the latter, the scuffle-hoe is still an indispensable time-saver.

There remains one task connected with gardening that is a bug-bear. That is hand-weeding. To get down on one's hands and knees, in the blistering hot dusty soil, with the perspiration trickling down into one's eyes, and pick small weedlets from among tender plantlets, is not a pleasant occupation. There are, however, several sorts of small weeders which lessen the work considerably. One or another of the common types will seem preferable, according to different conditions of soil and methods of work. Personally, I prefer the Lang's for most uses. The angle blade makes it possible to cut very near to small plants and between close-growing plants, while the strap over the back of a finger or thumb leaves the fingers free for weeding without dropping the instrument.

There are two things to be kept in mind about hand-weeding which will reduce this work to the minimum. First, never let the weeds get a start; for even if they do not increase in number, if they once smother the ground or crop, you will wish you had never heard of a garden. Second, do your hand-weeding while the surface soil is soft, when the weeds come out easily. A hard-crusted soil will double and treble the amount of labor required.

It would seem that it should be needless, when garden tools are such savers of labor, to suggest that they should be carefully kept, always bright and clean and sharp, and in repair. But such advice is needed, to judge by most of the tools one sees.

Always have a piece of cloth or old bag on hand where the garden tools are kept, and never put them away soiled and wet. Keep the cutting edges sharp. There is as much pleasure in trying to run a dull lawn-mower as in working with a rusty, battered hoe. Have an extra handle in stock in case of accident; they are not expensive. In selecting hand tools, always pick out those with handles in which the grain does not run out at the point where there will be much strain in using the tool. In rakes, hoes, etc., get the types with ferrule and shank one continuous piece, so as not to be annoyed with loose heads.

Spend a few cents to send for some implement catalogues. They will well repay careful perusal, even if you do not order this year. In these days of intensive advertising, the commercial catalogue often contains matter of great worth, in the gathering and presentation of which no expense has been spared.

FOR FIGHTING PLANT ENEMIES

The devices and implements used for fighting plant enemies are of two sorts:—

1. Those used to afford mechanical protection to the plants;

2. Those used to apply insecticides and fungicides.

Of the first the most useful is the covered frame. It consists usually of a wooden box, some eighteen inches to two feet square and about eight high, covered with glass, protecting cloth, mosquito netting or mosquito wire. The first two coverings have, of course, the additional advantage of retaining heat and protecting from cold, making it possible by their use to plant earlier than is otherwise safe. They are used extensively in getting an extra early and safe start with cucumbers, melons and the other vine vegetables.

Simpler devices for protecting newly-set plants, such as tomatoes or cabbage, from the cut-worm, are stiff, tin, cardboard or tar paper collars, which are made several inches high and large enough to be put around the stem and penetrate an inch or so into the soil.

For applying poison powders, such as dry Paris green, hellebore and tobacco dust, the home gardener should supply himself with a powder gun. If one must be restricted to a single implement, however, it will be best to get one of the hand-power, compressed-air sprayers—either a knapsack pump or a compressed-air sprayer—types of which are illustrated. These are used for applying wet sprays, and should be supplied with one of the several forms of mist-making nozzles, the non-cloggable automatic type being the best. For more extensive work a barrel pump, mounted on wheels, will be desirable, but one of the above will do a great deal of work in little time. Extension rods for use in spraying trees and vines may be obtained for either. For operations on a very small scale a good hand-syringe may be used, but as a general thing it will be best to invest a few dollars more and get a small tank sprayer, as this throws a continuous stream or spray and holds a much larger amount of the spraying solution. Whatever type is procured, get a brass machine—it will out-wear three or four of those made of cheaper metal, which succumbs very quickly to the, corroding action of the strong poisons and chemicals used in them.

Of implements for harvesting, beside the spade, prong-hoe and spading- fork already mentioned, very few are used in the small garden, as most of them need not only long rows to be economically used, but horse- power also. The onion harvester attachment for the double wheel hoe, costing $1.00, may be used with advantage in loosening onions, beets, turnips, etc., from the soil or for cutting spinach. Running the hand- plow close on either side of carrots, parsnips and other deep-growing vegetables will aid materially in getting them out. For fruit picking, with tall trees, the wire-fingered fruit-picker, secured to the end of a long handle, will be of great assistance, but with the modern method of using low-headed trees it will not be needed.

HOME VEGETABLE GARDENING

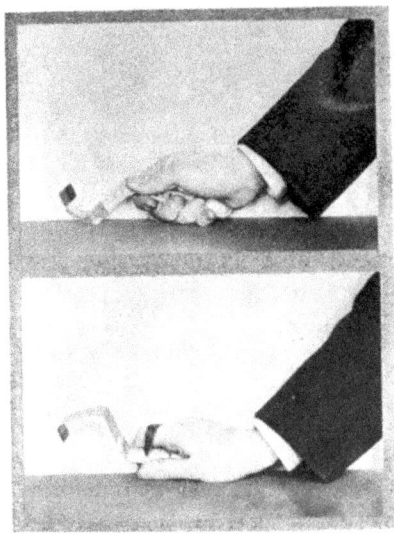

A type of hand-weeder that the author has found most convenient for general use. A strap extends over a finger or thumb, leaving the fingers free for weeding when desired. The cost is twenty cents

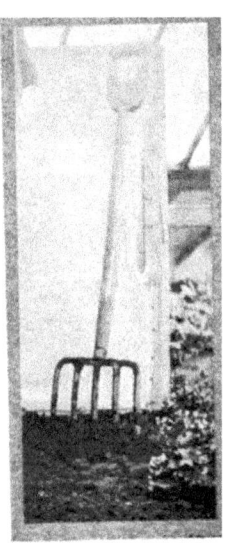

The spading-fork deserves to be better known for use in breaking up the soil

Another class of garden implements are those used in pruning—but where this is attended to properly from the start, a good sharp jack-knife and a pair of pruning shears (the English makes are the best, as they are in some things, when we are frank enough to confess the truth) will easily handle all the work of the kind necessary. Still another sort of garden device is that used for supporting the plants; such as stakes, trellises, wires, etc.

Altogether too little attention usually is given these, as with proper care in storing over winter they will not only last for years, but add greatly to the convenience of cultivation and to the neat appearance of the garden. Various contrivances are illustrated in the seed catalogues, and many may be home-made—such as a stake-trellis for supporting beans. As a final word to the intending purchaser of garden tools, I would say: first thoroughly investigate the different sorts available, and when buying, do not forget that a good tool or a well-made machine will be giving you satisfactory use long, long after the price is forgotten, while a poor one is a constant source of discomfort. Get good tools, and take good care of them. And let me repeat that a few dollars a year, judiciously spent, for tools afterward well cared for, will soon give you a very complete set, and add to your garden profit and pleasure.

Pulverize and level the soil by a backward-and-forward motion of the rake, not attempting to rake off all the small stones. Choose the bow-head rake rather than this pattern, as the former is stronger

Chapter 6

Manures and Fertilizers

To a very small extent garden vegetables get their food from the air. The amount obtained in this way however, is so infinitesimal that from the practical standpoint it need not be considered at all. Practically speaking, your vegetables must get all their food from the garden soil.

This important garden fact may seem self-evident, but, if one may judge by their practice, amateur gardeners very frequently fail to realize it. The professional gardener must come to realize it for the simple reason that if he does not he will go out of business. Without an abundant supply of suitable food it is just as impossible to grow good vegetables as it would be to train a winning football team on a diet of sweet cider and angel cake. Without plenty of plant food, all the care, coddling, coaxing, cultivating, spraying and worrying you may give will avail little. The soil must be rich or the garden will be poor.

Plant food is of as many kinds, or, more accurately speaking, in as many forms, as is food for human beings. But the first distinction to make in plant foods is that between available and non-available foods —that is, between foods which it is possible for the plant to use, and those which must undergo a change of some sort before the plant can take them up, assimilate them, and turn them into a healthy growth of foliage, fruit or root. It is just as readily possible for a plant to starve in a soil abounding in plant food, if that food is not available, as it would be for you to go unnourished in the midst of soups and tender meats if the latter were frozen solid.

Plants take all their nourishment in the form of soups, and very weak ones at that. Plant food to be available must be soluble to the action of the feeding root tubes; and unless it is available it might, as far as the present benefiting of your garden is concerned, just as well not be there at all. Plants take up their food through innumerable and microscopic feeding rootlets, which possess the power of absorbing moisture, and furnishing it, distributed by the plant juices, or sap, to stem, branch, leaf, flower and fruit. There is one startling fact which may help to fix these things in your memory: it takes from 300 to 500 pounds of water to furnish food for the building of one pound of dry plant matter. You can see why plant food is not of much use unless it is available; and it is not available unless it is soluble.

To have the ground feed you, you must first feed it. This is part of the "first course" for the author's garden patch

THE THEORY OF MANURING

The food of plants consists of chemical elements, or rather, of numerous substances which contain these elements in greater or less degrees. There is not room here to go into the interesting science of this matter. It is evident, however, as we have already seen that the plants must get their food from the soil, that there are but two sources for such food: it must either be in the soil already, or we must put it there. The practice of adding plant food to the soil is what is called manuring.

Apply nitrate of soda along the sides of rows, when the plants need an immediate stimulus. Do not get any on the leaves

Some of the chemical fertilizers are applied in the rows before the seeds are sown. Be careful to mix well with the soil before planting

The only three of the chemical elements mentioned which we need consider are: nitrogen, phosphoric acid, and potash. The average soil contains large amounts of all three, but they are for the most part in forms which are not available and, therefore, to that extent, may be at once dismissed from our consideration. (The non-available plant foods already in the soil may be released or made available to some extent by cultivation. See Chapter VII.) In practically every soil that has been cultivated and cropped, in long-settled districts, the amounts of nitrogen, phosphoric acid and potash which are immediately available will be too meager to produce a good crop of vegetables. It becomes absolutely necessary then, if one would have a really successful garden, no matter how small it is, to add plant foods to the soil abundantly. When you realize,

1. that the number of plant foods containing the three essential elements is almost unlimited,

2. that each contains them in different proportions and in differing degrees of availability,

3. that the amount of the available elements already in the soil varies greatly and is practically undeterminable, and

4. that different plants, and even different varieties of the same plant,

use these elements in widely differing proportions; then you begin to understand what a complex matter this question of manuring is and why it is so much discussed and so little understood. What a labyrinth it offers for any writer—to say nothing of the reader—to go astray in!

I have tried to present this matter clearly. If I have succeeded it may have been only to make the reader hopelessly discouraged of ever getting at anything definite in the question of enriching the soil. In that case my advice would be that, for the time being, he forget all about it. Fortunately, in the question of manuring, a little knowledge is not often a dangerous thing. Fortunately, too, your plants do not insist that you solve the food problem for them. Set a full table and they will help themselves and take the right dishes. The only thing to worry about is that of the three important foods mentioned (nitrogen, phosphoric acid and potash) there will not be enough: for it has been proved that when any one of these is exhausted the plant practically stops growth; it will not continue to "fill up" on the other two. Of course there is such a thing as going to extremes and wasting plant foods, even if it does not, as a rule, hurt the plants. If, however, the fertilizers and manures described in the following sections are applied as directed, and as mentioned in Chapter VII., good results will be certain, provided the seed, cultivation and season are right.

VARIOUS MANURES

The terms "manure" and "fertilizer" are used somewhat ambiguously and interchangeably. Using the former term in a broad sense—

as meaning any substance containing available plant food applied to the soil, we may say that manure is of two kinds: organic, such as stable manure, or decayed vegetable matter; and inorganic, such as potash salts, phosphatic rock and commercial mixed fertilizers. In a general way the term "fertilizer" applies to these inorganic manures, and I shall use it in this sense through the following text.

Between the organic manures, or "natural" manures as they are often called, and fertilizers there is a very important difference which should never be lost sight of. In theory, and as a chemical fact too, a bag of fertilizer may contain twice the available plant food of a ton of well-rotted manure; but out of a hundred practical gardeners ninety- nine—and probably one more—would prefer the manure. There is a reason why—two reasons, even if not one of the hundred gardeners could give them to you. First, natural manures have a decided physical effect upon most soils (altogether aside from the plant food they contain); and second, plants seem to have a preference as to the form in which their food elements are served to them. Fertilizers, on the other hand, are valuable only for the plant food they contain, and sometimes have a bad effect upon the physical condition of the soil.

When it comes right down to the practical question of what to put on your garden patch to grow big crops, nothing has yet been discovered that is better than the old reliable stand-by—well rotted, thoroughly fined stable or barnyard manure. Heed those adjectives! We have already seen that plant food which is not available might as well be, for our immediate purposes, at the North Pole. The plant food in "green" or fresh manure is not available, and does not become so until it is released by the decay of the organic matters therein. Now the time possible for growing a crop of garden vegetables is limited; in many instances it is only sixty to ninety days. The plants want their food ready at once; there is no time to be lost waiting for manure to rot in the soil. That is a slow process—especially so in clayey or heavy soils. So on your garden use only manure that is well rotted and broken up. On the other hand, see that it has not "fire-fanged" or burned out, as horse manure, if piled by itself and left, is very sure to do. If you keep any animals of your own, see that the various sorts of manure —excepting poultry manure, which is so rich that it is a good plan to keep it for special purposes—are mixed together and kept in a compact, built-up square heap, not a loose pyramidal pile. Keep it under cover and where it cannot wash out. If you have a pig or so, your manure will be greatly improved by the rooting, treading and mixing they will give it. If not, the pile should be turned from bottom to top and outside in and rebuilt, treading down firmly in the process, every month or two— applying water, but not soaking, if it has dried out in the meantime. Such manure will be worth two or three times as much, for garden purposes, as that left to burn or remain in frozen lumps. If you have to buy all your manure, get that which has been properly kept; and if you are not familiar with the condition in which it should be, get a disinterested gardener or farmer to select it for you. When possible, it will pay you to procure manure several months before you want to use it and work it over as suggested above. In buying manure keep in mind not what animals made it, but what food was fed —that is the important thing. For instance, the manure from highly-fed livery horses may be, weight for weight, worth three to five times that from cattle wintered over on poor hay, straw and a few roots.

There are other organic manures which it is sometimes possible for one to procure, such as refuse brewery hops, fish scraps and sewage, but they are as a rule out of the reach of, or objectionable for, the purposes of the home gardener.

There are, however, numerous things constantly going to waste about the small place, which should be converted into manure. Fallen leaves, grass clippings, vegetable tops and roots, green weeds, garbage, house slops, dish water, chip dirt from the wood-pile, shavings—anything that will rot away, should go into the compost heap. These should be saved, under cover if possible, in a compact heap and kept moist (never soaked) to help decomposition. To start the heap, gather up every available substance and make it into a pile with a few wheelbarrows full, or half a cartload, of fresh horse manure, treading the whole down firmly. Fermentation and decomposition will be quickly started. The heap should occasionally be forked over and restacked. Light dressings of lime, mixed in at such times, will aid thorough decomposition.

Wood ashes form another valuable manure which should be carefully saved. Beside the plant food contained, they have a most excellent effect upon the mechanical condition of almost every soil. Ashes should not be put in the compost heap, because there are special uses for them, such as dusting on squash or melon vines, or using on the onion bed, which makes it desirable to keep them separate. Wood ashes may frequently be bought for fifty cents a barrel, and at this price a few barrels for the home garden will be a good investment.

Coal ashes contain practically no available plant food, but are well worth saving to use on stiff soils, for paths, etc.

VALUE OF GREEN MANURING

Another source of organic manures, altogether too little appreciated, is what is termed "green manuring"—the plowing under of growing crops to enrich the land. Even in the home garden this system should be taken advantage of whenever possible. In farm practice, clover is the most valuable crop to use for this purpose, but on account of the length of time necessary to grow it, it is useful for the vegetable garden only when there is sufficient room to have clover growing on, say, one half-acre plot, while the garden occupies, for two years, another half-acre; and then changing the two about. This system will give an ideal garden soil, especially where it is necessary to rely for the most part upon chemical fertilizers.

There are, however, four crops valuable for green-manuring the garden, even where the same spot must be occupied year after year: rye, field corn, field peas (or cow peas in the south) and crimson clover. After the first of September, sow every foot of garden ground cleared of its last crop, with winter rye. Sow all ground cleared during August with crimson clover and buckwheat, and mulch the clover with rough manure after the buckwheat dies down. Sow field peas or corn on any spots that would otherwise remain unoccupied six weeks or more. All these are sown broadcast, on a freshly raked surface. Such a system will save a very large amount of plant food which otherwise would be lost, will convert unavailable plant food into available forms while you wait for the next crop, and add humus to the soil—concerning the importance of which see Chapter VII.

CHEMICAL FERTILIZERS

I am half tempted to omit entirely any discussion of chemical fertilizers: to give a list of them, tell how to apply them, and let the why and wherefore go. It is, however, such an important subject, and the home gardener will so frequently have to rely almost entirely upon their use, that probably it will be best to explain the subject as thoroughly as I can do it in very limited space. I shall try to give the theory of scientific chemical manuring in one paragraph.

We have already seen that the soil contains within itself some available plant food. We can determine by chemical analysis the exact amounts of the various plant foods—nitrogen, phosphoric acid, potash, etc.—which a crop of any vegetable will remove from the soil. The idea in scientific chemical manuring is to add to the available plant foods already in the soil just enough more to make the resulting amounts equal to the quantities of the various elements used by the crop grown. In other words:

$$\left.\begin{array}{l}\text{Available plant food elements in the soil, plus} \\ \text{Available chemical food elements supplied in fertilizers}\end{array}\right\} = \text{Amounts of food elements in matured crop}$$

That was the theory—a very pretty and profound one! The discoverers of it imagined that all agriculture would be revolutionized; all farm and garden practice reduced to an exact science; all older theories of husbandry and tillage thrown by the heels together upon the scrap heap of outworn things. Science was to solve at one fell swoop all the age-old problems of agriculture. And the whole thing was all right in every way but one—it didn't work. The unwelcome and obdurate fact remained that a certain number of pounds of nitrogen, phosphoric acid and potash—about thirty-three—in a ton of good manure would grow bigger crops than would the same number of pounds of the same elements in a bag of chemical fertilizer.

Nevertheless this theory, while it failed as the basis of an exact agricultural science, has been developed into an invaluable guide for using all manures, and especially concentrated chemical manures. And the above facts, if I have presented them clearly, will assist the home gardener in solving the fertilizer problems which he is sure to encounter.

VARIOUS FERTILIZERS

What are termed the raw materials from which the universally known "mixed fertilizers" are made up, are organic or inorganic substances which contain nitrogen, phosphoric acid or potash in fairly definite amounts.

Some of these can be used to advantage by themselves. Those practical for use by the home gardener, I mention. The special uses to which they are adapted will be mentioned in Part Two, under the vegetables for which they are valuable.

GROUND BONE is rich in phosphate and lasts a long time; what is called "raw bone" is the best "Bone dust" or "bone flour" is finely pulverized; it will produce quick results, but does not last as long as the coarser forms.

COTTON-SEED MEAL is one of the best nitrogenous fertilizers for garden crops. It is safer than nitrate of soda in the hands of the inexperienced gardener, and decays very quickly in the soil.

PERUVIAN GUANO, in the pure form, is now practically out of the market. Lower grades, less rich in nitrogen especially, are to be had; and also "fortified" guano, in which chemicals are added to increase the content of nitrogen. It is good for quick results.

NITRATE OF SODA, when properly handled, frequently produces wonderful results in the garden, particularly upon quick-growing crops. It is the richest in nitrogen of any chemical generally used, and a great stimulant to plant growth. When used alone it is safest to mix with an equal bulk of light dirt or some other filler. If applied pure, be sure to observe the following rules or you may burn your plants:

1. Pulverize all lumps;

2. See that none of it lodges upon the foliage;

3. Never apply when there is moisture upon the plants;

4. Apply in many small doses—say 10 to 20 pounds at a time for 50 x 100 feet of garden.

It should be put on so sparingly as to be barely visible; but its presence will soon be denoted by the moist spot, looking like a big rain drop, which each particle of it makes in the dry soil. Nitrate of soda may also be used safely in solution, at the rate of 1 pound to 12 gallons of water. I describe its use thus at length because I consider it the most valuable single chemical which the gardener has at command.

MURIATE and SULPHATE OF POTASH are also used by themselves as sources of potash, but as a general thing it will be best to use them in combination with other chemicals as described under "Home Mixing."

LIME will be of benefit to most soils. It acts largely as an indirect fertilizer, helping to release other food elements already in the soil, but in non-available forms. It should be applied once in three to five years, at the rate of 75 to 100 bushels per acre, after plowing, and thoroughly harrowed in. Apply as long before planting as possible, or in the fall.

MIXED FERTILIZERS

Mixed fertilizers are of innumerable brands, and for sale everywhere. It is little use to pay attention to the claims made for them. Even where the analysis is guaranteed, the ordinary gardener has no way of knowing that the contents of his few bags are what they are labeled. The best you can do, however, is to buy on the basis of analysis, not of price per ton—usually the more you pay per bag, the cheaper you are really buying your actual plant food. Send to the Experiment Station in your State and ask for the last bulletin on fertilizer values. It will give a list of the brands sold throughout the State, the retail price per ton, and the actual value of plant foods contained in a ton. Then buy the brand in which you will apparently get the greatest value.

For garden crops the mixed fertilizer you use should contain (about):

$$\left.\begin{array}{l}\text{Nitrogen, 4 per cent.}\\ \text{Phosphoric acid, 8 per cent.}\\ \text{Potash, 10 per cent.}\end{array}\right\} = \begin{array}{c}\text{Basic formula}\\ \text{for}\\ \text{Garden crops}\end{array}$$

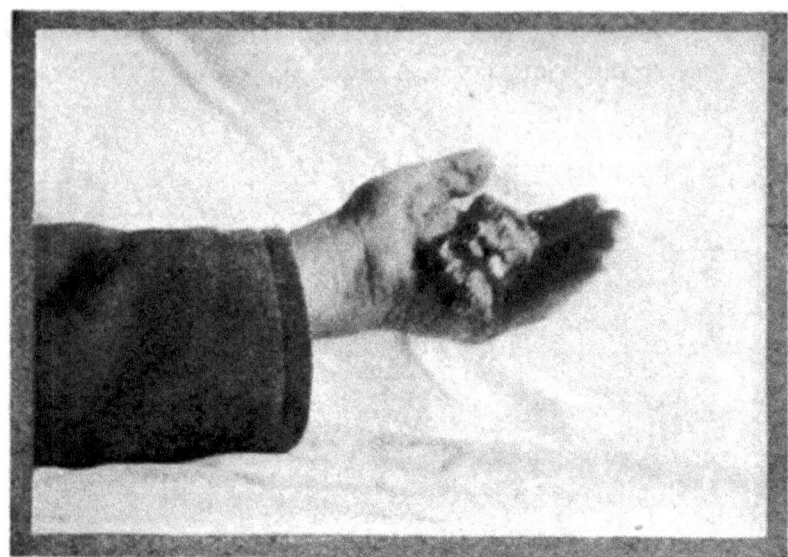

If the soil after rain compresses into a pasty compact mass, turn to another spot for your garden site

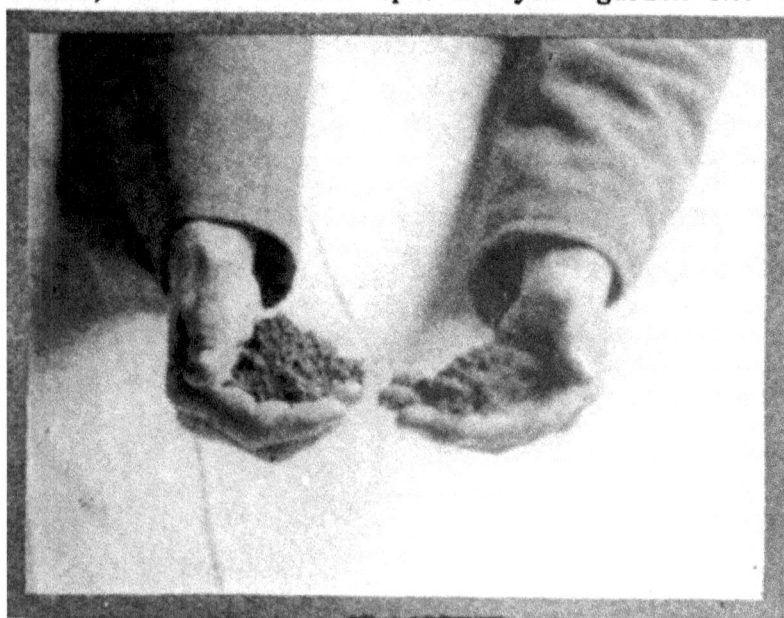

If the compressed ball of earth crumbles apart in the hands when released, it is good garden loam.

Sow small seeds directly from the packet, shaking them directly into the drill when there is no wind. Cover at once

In order to avoid washing out the seeds by watering, cover the flat with burlap to ease the force of the water

If applied alone, use at the rate of 1000 to 1500 pounds per acre. If with manure, less, in proportion to the amount of the latter used.

By "basic formula" (see above) is meant one which contains the plant foods in the proportion which all garden crops must have. Particular crops may need additional amounts of one or more of the three elements, in order to attain their maximum growth. Such extra feeding is usually supplied by top dressings, during the season of growth. The extra food beneficial to the different vegetables will be mentioned in the cultural directions in Part Two.

HOME MIXING

If you look over the Experiment Station report mentioned above, you will notice that what are called "home mixtures" almost invariably show a higher value compared to the cost than any regular brand. In some cases the difference is fifty per cent. This means that you can buy the raw chemicals and make up your own mixtures cheaper than you can buy mixed fertilizers. More than that, it means you will have purer mixtures. More than that, it means you will have on hand the materials for giving your crops the special feeding mentioned above. The idea widely prevails, thanks largely to the fertilizer companies, that home mixing cannot be practically done, especially upon a small scale. From both information and personal experience I know the contrary to be the case. With a tight floor or platform, a square-pointed shovel and a coarse wire screen, there is absolutely nothing impractical about it. The important thing is to see that all ingredients are evenly and thoroughly mixed. A scale for weighing will also be a convenience. Further information may be had from the firms which sell raw materials, or from your Experiment Station.

APPLYING MANURES

The matter of properly applying manure, even on the small garden, is also of importance. In amount, from fifteen to twenty-five cords, or 60 to 100 cartloads, will not be too much; although if fertilizers are used to help out, the manure may be decreased in proportion. If possible, take it from the heap in which it has been rotting, and spread evenly over the soil immediately before plowing. If actively fermenting, it will lose by being exposed to wind and sun. If green, or in cold weather, it may be spread and left until plowing is done. When plowing, it should be completely covered under, or it will give all kinds of trouble in sowing and cultivating.

Fertilizers should be applied, where used to supplement manure or in place of it, at from 500 to 1500 pounds per acre, according to grade and other conditions. It is sown on broadcast, after plowing, care being taken to get it evenly distributed. This may be assured by sowing half while going across the piece, and the other half while going lengthwise of it. When used as a starter, or for top dressings—as mentioned in connection with the basic formula—it may be put in the hill or row at time of planting, or applied on the surface and worked in during the growth of the plants. In either case, especially with highly concentrated chemicals, care must be taken to mix them thoroughly with the soil and to avoid burning the tender roots.

This chapter is longer than I wanted to make it, but the problem of how best to enrich the soil is the most difficult one in the whole business of gardening, and the degree of your success in growing vegetables will be measured pretty much by the extent to which you master it. You cannot do it at one reading. Re-read this chapter, and when you understand the several subjects mentioned, in the brief way which limited space made necessary, pursue them farther in one of the several comprehensive books on the subject. It will well repay all the time you spend upon it. Because, from necessity, there has been so much of theory mixed up with the practical in this chapter, I shall very briefly recapitulate the directions for just what to do, in order that the subject of manuring may be left upon the same practical basis governing the rest of the book.

To make your garden rich enough to grow big crops, buy the most thoroughly worked over and decomposed manure you can find. If it is from grain-fed animals, and if pigs have run on it, it will be better yet. If possible, buy enough to put on at the rate of about twenty cords to the acre; if not, supplement the manure, which should be plowed under, with 500 to 1500 pounds of high-grade mixed fertilizer (analyzing nitrogen four per cent., phosphoric acid eight per cent., potash ten per cent.)—the quantity in proportion to the amount of manure used, and spread on broadcast after plowing and thoroughly harrowed in. In addition to this general enrichment of the soil, suitable quantities of nitrate of soda, for nitrogen; bone dust (or acid phosphate), for phosphoric acid; and sulphate of potash, for potash, should be bought for later dressings, as suggested in cultural directions for the various crops.

If the instructions in the above paragraph are followed out you may rest assured that your vegetables will not want for plant food and that, if other conditions are favorable, you will have maximum crops.

Chapter 7

The Soil and Its Preparation

Having considered, as thoroughly as the limited space available permitted, the matter of plant foods, we must proceed to the equally important one of how properly to set the table, on or rather in, which they must be placed, before the plants can use them.

As was noted in the first part of the preceding chapter, most tillable soils contain the necessary plant food elements to a considerable extent, but only in a very limited degree in available forms. They are locked up in the soil larder, and only after undergoing physical and chemical changes may be taken up by the feeding roots of plants. They are unlocked only by the disintegration and decomposition of the soil particles, under the influence of cultivation—or mechanical breaking up—and the access of water, air and heat.

The great importance of the part the soil must play in every garden operation is therefore readily seen. In the first place, it is required to furnish all the plant food elements—some seven in number, beside the three, nitrogen, phosphoric acid and potash, already mentioned. In the second, it must hold the moisture in which these foods must be either dissolved or suspended before plant roots can take them up.

The soil is naturally classified in two ways: first, as to the amount of plant food contained; second, as to its mechanical condition—the relative proportions of sand, decomposed stone and clay, of which it is made up, and also the degree to which it has been broken up by cultivation.

The approximate amount of available plant food already contained in the soil can be determined satisfactorily only by experiment. As before stated, however, almost without exception they will need liberal manuring to produce good garden crops. I shall therefore not go further into the first classification of soils mentioned.

Of soils, according to their variation in mechanical texture, I shall mention only the three which the home gardener is likely to encounter. Rocks are the original basis of all soils, and according to the degree of fineness to which they have been reduced, through centuries of decomposition by air, moisture and frost, they are known as gravelly, sandy or clayey soils.

CLAY SOILS are stiff, wet, heavy and usually "cold." For garden purposes, until properly transformed, they hold too much water, are difficult to handle, and are "late." But even if there be no choice but a clay soil for the home garden, the gardener need not be discouraged. By proper treatment it may be brought into excellent condition for growing vegetables, and will produce some sorts, such as celery, better than any warm, light, "garden" soil. The first thing to do with the clay soil garden, is to have it thoroughly drained. For the small amount of ground usually required for a home garden, this will entail no great expense. Under ordinary conditions, a half-acre garden could be under-drained for from $25 to $50—probably nearer the first figure. The drains—round drain tile, with collars—should be placed at least three feet deep, and if they can be put four, it will be much better. The lines should be, for the former depth, twenty to thirty feet apart, according to character of the soil; if four feet deep, they will accomplish just as much if put thirty to fifty feet apart—so it pays to put them in deep. For small areas 2-1/2-inch land tile will do. The round style gives the best satisfaction and will prove cheapest in the end. The outlet should of course be at the lowest point of land, and all drains, main and laterals, should fall slightly, but without exception, toward this point. Before undertaking to put in the drains, even on a small area, it will pay well to read some good book on the subject, such as Draining for Profit and Draining for Health, by Waring.

But drain—if your land requires it. It will increase the productiveness of your garden at least 50 to 100 per cent.—and such an increase, as you can readily see, will pay a very handsome annual dividend on the cost of draining. Moreover, the draining system, if properly put in, will practically never need renewal.

On land that has a stiff or clay sub-soil, it will pay well to break this up—thus making it more possible for the water to soak down through the surface soil rapidly—by using the sub-soil plow. (See Chapter V.)

The third way to improve clay soils is by using coarse vegetable manures, large quantities of stable, manures, ashes, chips, sawdust, sand, or any similar materials, which will tend to break up and lighten the soil mechanically. Lime and land plaster are also valuable, as they cause chemical changes which tend to break up clayey soils.

The fourth thing to do in treating a garden of heavy soil is to plow, ridging up as much as possible, in the fall, thus leaving the soil exposed to the pulverizing influences of weather and frost. Usually it will not need replowing in the spring. If not plowed until the spring, care should be taken not to plow until it has dried out sufficiently to crumble from the plow, instead of making a wet, pasty furrow.

The owner of a clayey garden has one big consolation. It will not let his plant food go to waste. It will hold manures and fertilizers incorporated with it longer than any other soil.

SANDY SOIL is, as the term implies, composed largely of sand, and is the reverse of clay soil. So, also, with the treatment. It should be so handled as to be kept as compact as possible. The use of a heavy roller, as frequently as possible, will prove very beneficial. Sowing or planting should follow immediately after plowing, and fertilizers or manures should be applied only immediately before.

If clay soil is obtainable nearby, a small area of sandy soil, such as is required for the garden, can be made into excellent soil by the addition of the former, applied as you would manure. Plow the garden in the fall and spread the clay soil on evenly, harrowing in with a disc in the spring. The result will be as beneficial as that of an equal dressing of good manure—and will be permanent.

It is one of the valuable qualities of lime, and also of gypsum to even a greater extent, that while it helps a clay soil, it is equally valuable for a sandy one. The same is true of ashes and of the organic manures—especially of green manuring. Fertilizers, on sandy soils, where they will not long be retained, should be applied only immediately before planting, or as top and side dressing during growth.

Sandy soil in the garden will produce early and quick results, and is especially adapted to melons, cucumbers, beans and a number of the other garden vegetables.

GRAVELLY SOIL is generally less desirable than either of the others; it has the bad qualities of sandy soil and not the good ones of clay, besides being poorer in plant food. (Calcareous, or limestone pebble, soils are an exception, but they are not widely encountered.) They are not suited for garden work, as tillage harms rather than helps them.

THE IDEAL GARDEN SOIL is what is known as a "rich, sandy loam," at least eight inches deep; if it is eighteen it will be better. It contains the proper proportions of both sand and clay, and further has been put into the best of mechanical condition by good tilth.

That last word brings us to a new and very important matter. "In good tilth" is a condition of the soil difficult to describe, but a state that the gardener comes soon to recognize. Ground, continually and properly cultivated, comes soon to a degree of fineness and lightness at once recognizable. Rain is immediately absorbed by it, and does not stand upon the surface; it does not readily clog or pack down; it is crumbly and easily worked; and until your garden is brought to this condition you cannot attain the greatest success from your efforts. I emphasized "properly cultivated." That means that the soil must be kept well supplied with humus, or decomposed vegetable matter, either by the application of sufficient quantities of organic manures, or by green manuring, or by "resting under grass," which produces a similar result from the amount of roots and stubble with which the soil is filled when the sod is broken up. Only by this supply of humus can the garden be kept in that light, friable, spongy condition which is absolutely essential to luxuriant vegetable growth.

PREPARING THE SOIL

Unless your garden be a very small one indeed, it will pay to have it plowed rather than dug up by hand. If necessary, arrange the surrounding fence as suggested in the accompanying diagram, to make possible the use of a horse for plowing and harrowing. (As suggested in the chapter on Implements), if there is not room for a team, the one- horse plow, spring-tooth and spike-tooth cultivators, can do the work in very small spaces.

If however the breaking up of the garden must be done by hand, have it done deeply—down to the sub-soil, or as deep as the spading-fork will go. And have it done thoroughly, every spadeful turned completely and every inch dug. It is hard work, but it must not be slighted.

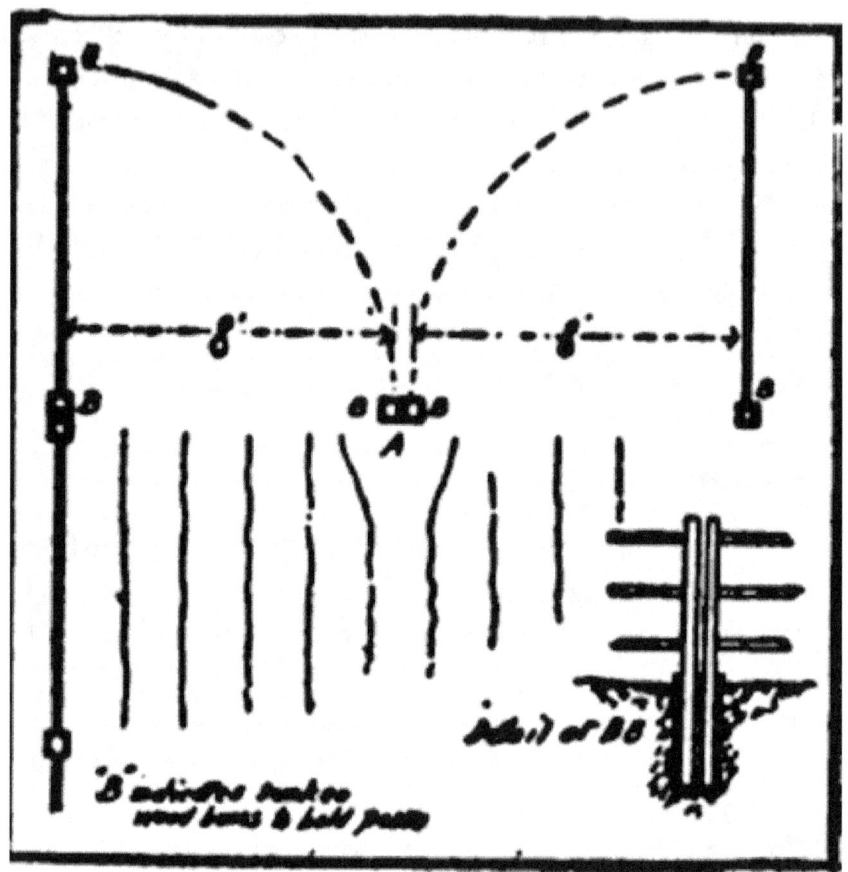

PLOWING

If the garden can be plowed in the fall, by all means have it done. If it is in sod, it must be done at that time if good results are to be secured the following season. In this latter case, plow a shallow furrow four to six inches deep and turning flat, as early as possible in the fall, turning under a coating of horse manure, or dressing of lime, and then going over it with a smoothing-harrow or the short blades of the Acme, to fill in all crevices. The object of the plowing is to get the sods rotted thoroughly before the following spring; then apply manure and plow deeply, six to twelve inches, according to the soil.

Where the old garden is to be plowed up, if there has not been time to get in one of the cover crops suggested elsewhere in this text, plow as late as possible, and in ridges. If the soil is light and sandy, fall plowing will not be advisable.

In beginning the spring work it is customary to put on the manure and plow but once. But the labor of double plowing will be well repaid, especially on a soil likely to suffer from drouth, if the ground be plowed once, deeply, before the manure is spread on, and then cross- plowed just sufficiently to turn the manure well under—say five or six inches. On stiff lands, and especially for root crops, it will pay if possible to have the sub-soil plow follow the regular plow. This is, of course, for thoroughly rotted and fined manure; if coarse, it had better be put under at one plowing, making the best of a handicap. If you have arranged to have your garden plowed "by the job," be on hand to see that no shirking is done, by taking furrows wider than the plow can turn completely; it is possible to "cut and cover" so that the surface of a piece will look well enough, when in reality it is little better than half plowed.

HARROWING

That is the first step toward the preparation of a successful garden out of the way. Next comes the harrowing; if the soil after plowing is at all stiff and lumpy, get a disc-harrow if you can; on clayey soils a "cut-a-way" (see Implements). On the average garden soil, however, the Acme will do the work of pulverizing in fine shape.

If, even after harrowing, the soil remains lumpy, have the man who is doing your work get a horse-roller somewhere, and go over the piece with that. The roller should be used also on very sandy and light soils, after the first harrowing (or after the plowing, if the land turns over mellow) to compact it. To follow the first harrowing (or the roller) use a smoothing-harrow, the Acme set shallow, or a "brush."

FINING.

This treatment will reduce to a minimum the labor of finally preparing the seed- or plant-bed with the iron rake (or, on large gardens, with the Meeker harrow). After the finishing touches, the soil should be left so even and smooth that you can with difficulty bring yourself to step on it. Get it "like a table"—and then you are ready to begin gardening.

Whatever implements are used, do not forget the great importance of making the soil thoroughly fine, not only at the surface, but as far as possible below Even under the necessity of repetition. I want to emphasize this again by stating the four chief benefits, of this thorough pulverization: First, it adds materially in making the plant foods in the soil available for use; secondly, it induces the growing plants to root deeply, and thus to a greater extent to escape the drying influence of the sun; thirdly, it enables the soil to absorb rain evenly, where it falls, which would otherwise either run off and be lost altogether, or collect in the lower parts of the garden; and last, and most important, it enables the soil to retain moisture thus stored, as in a subterranean storage tank, but where the plants can draw upon it, long after carelessly prepared and shallow soils are burning up in the long protracted drouths which we seem to be increasingly certain of getting during the late summer.

Prepare your garden deeply, thoroughly, carefully, in addition to making it rich, and you may then turn to those more interesting operations outlined in the succeeding sections, with the well founded assurance that your thought and labor will be rewarded by a garden so remarkably more successful than the average garden is, that all your extra pains-taking will be richly repaid.

Part 2

Vegetables

Chapter 8

Starting the Plants

This beautifully prepared garden spot—or rather the plant food in it— is to be transformed into good things for your table, through the ever wonderful agency of plant growth. The thread of life inhering in the tiniest seed, in the smallest plant, is the magic wand that may transmute the soil's dull metal into the gold of flower and fruit.

All the thought, care and expense described in the preceding chapters are but to get ready for the two things from which your garden is to spring, in ways so deeply hidden that centuries of the closest observation have failed to reveal their inner workings. Those two are seeds and plants. (The sticklers for technical exactness will here take exception, calling our attention to tubers, bulbs, corns and numerous other taverns where plant life puts up overnight, between growth and growth, but for our present purpose we need not mind them.)

The plants which you put out in your garden will have been started under glass from seed, so that, indirectly, everything depends on the seed. Good seeds, and true, you must have if your garden is to attain that highest success which should be our aim. Seeds vary greatly—very much more so than the beginner has any conception of. There are three essentials; if seeds fail in any one of them, they will be rendered next to useless. First, they must be true; selected from good types of stock and true to name; then they must have been good, strong, plump seeds, full of life and gathered from healthy plants; and finally, they must be fresh.

[Footnote: See table later this chapter] It is therefore of vital importance that you procure the best seeds that can be had, regardless of cost. Poor seeds are dear at any price; you cannot afford to accept them as a gift. It is, of course, impossible to give a rule by which to buy good seed, but the following suggestions will put you on the safe track. First, purchase only of some reliable mail-order house; do not be tempted, either by convenience or cheapness, to buy the gaily lithographed packets displayed in grocery and hardware stores at planting time—as a rule they are not reliable; and what you want for your good money is good seed, not cheap ink. Second, buy of seedsmen who make a point of growing and testing their own seed. Third, to begin with, buy from several houses and weed out to the one which proves, by actual results, to be the most reliable. Another good plan is to purchase seed of any particular variety from the firm that makes a leading specialty of it; in many cases these specialties have been introduced by these firms and they grow their own supplies of these seeds; they will also be surer of being true to name and type.

Good plants are, in proportion to the amounts used, just as important as good seed—and of course you cannot afford losing weeks of garden usefulness by growing entirely from seed sown out-doors. Beets, cabbage, cauliflower, lettuce, tomatoes, peppers, egg-plant, and for really efficient gardening, also onions, corn, melons, celery, lima beans, cucumbers, and squash, will all begin their joyous journey toward the gardener's table several weeks before they get into the garden at all. They will all be started under glass and have attained a good, thrifty, growing size before they are placed in the soil we have been so carefully preparing for them. It is next to impossible to describe a "good" vegetable plant, but he who gardens will come soon to distinguish between the healthy, short-jointed, deep-colored plant which is ready to take hold and grow, and the soft, flabby (or too succulent) drawn-up growth of plants which have been too much pampered, or dwarfed, weazened specimens which have been abused and starved; he will learn that a dozen of the former will yield more than fifty of the latter. Plants may be bought of the florist or market gardener. If so, they should be personally selected, sometime ahead, and gotten some few days before needed for setting out, so that you may be sure to have them properly "hardened off," and in the right degree of moisture, for transplanting, as will be described later.

By far the more satisfactory way, however, is to grow them yourself. You can then be sure of having the best of plants in exactly the quantities and varieties you want. They will also be on hand when conditions are just right for setting them out.

For the ordinary garden, all the plants needed may be started successfully in hotbeds and cold-frames. The person who has had no experience with these has usually an exaggerated idea of their cost and of the skill required to manage them. The skill is not as much a matter of expert knowledge as of careful regular care, daily. Only a few minutes a day, for a few sash, but every day. The cost need be but little, especially if one is a bit handy with tools. The sash which serves for the cover, and is removable, is the important part of the structure. Sash may be had, ready glazed and painted, at from $2.50 to $3.50 each, and with care they will last ten or even twenty years, so you can see at once that not a very big increase in the yield of your garden will be required to pay interest on the investment. Or you can buy the sash unglazed, at a proportionately lower price, and put the glass in yourself, if you prefer to spend a little more time and less money. However, if you are not familiar with the work, and want only a few sash, I would advise purchasing the finished article. In size they are three feet by six.

Frames upon which to put the sash covering may also be bought complete, but here there is a chance to save money by constructing your own frames—the materials required, being 2x4 in. lumber for posts, and inch-boards; or better, if you can easily procure them, plank 2 x 12 in.

So far as these materials go the hotbed and coldframe are alike. The difference is that while the coldframe depends for its warmth upon catching and holding the heat of the sun's rays, the hotbed is artificially heated by fermenting manure, or in rare instances, by hot water or steam pipes.

How one home-owner solved the problem of securing an effective and unobtrusive place for raising seedlings in the early spring. Unfortunately, not many houses have a roof of this form, but perhaps there is some other place about your own home in which you can build a garden under glass

Whether your place is one of several acres, or merely a plot 50x150 feet, you should have a hotbed or a coldframe to gain a month on summer every year and to carry over through the winter tender plants that cannot survive exposure

In constructing the hotbed there are two methods used; either by placing the frames on top of the manure heap or by putting the manure within the frames. The first method has the advantage of permitting the hotbed to be made upon frozen ground, when required in the spring. The latter, which is the better, must be built before the ground freezes, but is more economical of manure. The manure in either case should be that of grain-fed horses, and if a small amount of straw bedding, or leaves—not more, however, than one-third of the latter—be mixed among it, so much the better. Get this manure several days ahead of the time wanted for use and prepare by stacking in a compact, tramped-down heap. Turn it over after three or four days, and re-stack, being careful to put the former top and sides of the pile now on the inside.

Having now ready the heating apparatus and the superstructure of our miniature greenhouse, the building of it is a very simple matter. If the ground is frozen, spread the manure in a low, flat heap—nine or ten feet side, a foot and a half deep, and as long as the number of sash to be used demands—a cord of manure thus furnishing a bed for about three sash, not counting for the ends of the string or row. This heap should be well trodden down and upon it should be placed or built the box or frame upon which the sash are to rest. In using this method it will be more convenient to have the frame made up beforehand and ready to place upon the manure, as shown in one of the illustrations. This should be at least twelve inches high at the front and some half a foot higher at the back. Fill in with at least four inches—better six —of good garden soil containing plenty of humus, that it may allow water to soak through readily.

The other method is to construct the frames on the ground before severe freezing, and in this case the front should be at least twenty-four inches high, part of which—not more than half—may be below the ground level. The 2 x 12 in. planks, when used, are handled as follows: stakes are driven in to support the back plank some two or three inches above the ground,—which should, of course, be level. The front plank is sunk two or three inches into the ground and held upright by stakes on the outside, nailed on. Remove enough dirt from inside the frame to bank up the planks about halfway on the outside. When this banking has frozen to a depth of two or three inches, cover with rough manure or litter to keep frost from striking through. The manure for heating should be prepared as above and put in to the depth of a foot, trodden down, first removing four to six inches of soil to be put back on top of the manure,—a cord of the latter, in this case, serving seven sashes. The vegetable to be grown, and the season and climate, will determine the depth of manure required—it will be from one to two feet,—the latter depth seldom being necessary. It must not be overlooked that this manure, when spent for heating purposes, is still as good as ever to enrich the garden, so that the expense of putting it in and removing it from the frames is all that you can fairly charge up against your experiment with hotbeds, if you are interested to know whether they really pay.

The exposure for the hotbeds should be where the sun will strike most directly and where they will be sheltered from the north. Put up a fence of rough boards, five or six feet high, or place the frames south of some building.

The coldframe is constructed practically as in the hotbed, except that if manure is used at all it is for the purpose of enriching the soil where lettuce, radishes, cucumbers or other crops are to be grown to maturity in it.

If one can put up even a very small frame greenhouse, it will be a splendid investment both for profit and for pleasure. The cost is lower than is generally imagined, where one is content with a home-made structure. Look into it.

PREPARING THE SOIL

All this may seem like a lot of trouble to go to for such a small thing as a packet of seed. In reality it is not nearly so much trouble as it sounds, and then, too, this is for the first season only, a well-built frame lasting for years—forever, if you want to take a little more time and make it of concrete instead of boards.

But now that the frame is made, how to use it is the next question.

The first consideration must be the soil. It should be rich, light, friable. There are some garden loams that will do well just as taken up, but as a rule better results will be obtained where the soil is made up specially as follows: rotted sods two parts, old rotted manure one part, and enough coarse sand added to make the mixture fine and crumbly, so that, even when moist, it will fall apart when pressed into a ball in the hand. Such soil is best prepared by cutting out sod, in the summer, where the grass is green and thick, indicating a rich soil. Along old fences or the roadside where the wash has settled will be good places to get limited quantities. Those should be cut with considerable soil and stacked, grassy sides together, in layers in a compost pile. If the season proves very dry, occasionally soak the heap through. In late fall put in the cellar, or wherever solid freezing will not take place, enough to serve for spring work under glass. The amount can readily be calculated; soil for three sash, four inches deep, for instance, would take eighteen feet or a pile three feet square and two feet high. The fine manure (and sand, if necessary) may be added in the fall or when using in the spring. Here again it may seem to the amateur that unnecessary pains are being taken. I can but repeat what has been suggested all through this book, that it will require but little more work to do the thing the best way as long as one is doing it at all, and the results will be not only better, but practically certain—and that is a tremendously important point about all gardening operations.

SOWING THE SEED

Having now our frames provided and our soil composed properly and good strong tested seed on hand, we are prepared to go about the business of growing our plants with a practical certainty of success—a much more comfortable feeling than if, because something or other had been but half done, we must anxiously await results and the chances of having the work we had put into the thing go, after all, for nothing.

The seed may be sown either directly in the soil or in "flats." Flats are made as follows: Get from your grocer a number of cracker boxes, with the tops. Saw the boxes lengthwise into sections, a few two inches deep and the rest three. One box will make four or five such sections, for two of which bottoms will be furnished by the bottom and top of the original box. Another box of the same size, knocked apart, will furnish six bottoms more to use for the sections cut from the middle of the box. The bottoms of all, if tight, should have, say, five three- quarter-inch holes bored in them to allow any surplus water to drain off from the soil. The shallow flats may be used for starting the seed and the three-inch ones for transplanting. Where sowing but a small quantity of each variety of seed, the flats will be found much more convenient than sowing directly in the soil—and in the case of their use, of course, the soil on top of the manure need be but two or three inches deep and not especially prepared.

A coldframe need by no means be an unsightly garden accessory. This frame is tucked away in a southeastern **angle of the house**

HOME VEGETABLE GARDENING

A flat of cabbage just breaking ground. If the soil is crusted and makes "tents," break it through by watering

Cabbage almost ready for transplanting. The first leaves are just showing

Where the seed is to go directly into the frames, the soil described above is, of course, used. But when in flats, to be again transplanted, the soil for the first sowing will be better for having no manure in it, the idea being to get the hardest, stockiest growth possible. Soil for the flats in which the seeds are to be planted should be, if possible, one part sod, one part chip dirt or leaf mold, and one part sand.

The usual way of handling the seed flats is to fill each about one-third full of rough material—screenings, small cinders or something similar—and then fill the box with the prepared earth, which should first be finely sifted. This, after the seeds are sown, should be copiously watered—with a fine rose spray, or if one has not such, through a folded bag to prevent the washing of the soil.

Here is another way which I have used recently and, so far, with one hundred per cent, certainty of results. Last fall, when every bit of soil about my place was ash dry, and I had occasion to start immediately some seeds that were late in reaching me, my necessity mothered the following invention, an adaptation of the principle of sub-irrigation. To have filled the flats in the ordinary way would not have done, as it would have been impossible ever to wet the soil through without making a solid mud cake of it, in which seeds would have stood about as good a chance of doing anything as though not watered at all. I filled the flats one-third full of sphagnum moss, which was soaked, then to within half an inch of the top with soil, which was likewise soaked, and did not look particularly inviting. The flats were then filled level-full of the dust-dry soil, planted, and put in partial shade. Within half a day the surface soil had come to just the right degree of moisture, soaked up from below, and there was in a few days more a perfect stand of seedlings. I have used this method in starting all my seedlings this spring—some forty thousand, so far—only using soil screenings, mostly small pieces of decayed sod, in place of the moss and giving a very light watering in the surface to make it compact and to swell the seed at once. Two such flats are shown just ready to transplant. The seedlings illustrated in the upper flat had received just two waterings since being planted.

Where several hundred or more plants of each variety are wanted, sow the seed broadcast as evenly as possible and fairly thick—one ounce of cabbage, for instance, to three to five 13 x 19 inch flats. If but a few dozen, or a hundred, are wanted, sow in rows two or three inches apart, being careful to label each correctly. Before sowing, the soil should be pressed firmly into the corners of the flats and leveled off perfectly smooth with a piece of board or shingle. Press the seed evenly into the soil with a flat piece of board, cover it lightly, one- eighth to one-quarter inch, with sifted soil, press down barely enough to make smooth, and water with a very fine spray, or through burlap.

For the next two days the flats can go on a pretty hot surface, if one is available, such as hot water or steam pipes, or top of a boiler, but if these are not convenient, directly into the frame, where the temperature should be kept as near as possible to that indicated in the following table.

In from two to twelve days, according to temperature and variety, the little seedlings will begin to appear. In case the soil has not been made quite friable enough, they will sometimes "raise the roof" instead of breaking through. If so, see that the surface is broken up at once, with the fingers and a careful watering, as otherwise many of the little plants may become bent and lanky in a very short time.

From now on until they are ready to transplant, a period of some three or four weeks, is the time when they will most readily be injured by neglect. There are things you will have to look out for, and your attention must be regular to the matters of temperature, ventilation and moisture.

Vegetable	Date to Sow	Seed Will Keep (about)	Best Temperature to Germinate (about)
Beets	Feb. 15–Apr. 1	5 years	55 degrees
Broccoli	Feb. 15–Apr. 1	5 "	55 degrees
Brussels Sprouts	Feb. 15–Apr. 1	7 "	55 degrees
Cabbage	Feb. 1–Apr. 1	7 "	55 degrees
Cauliflower	Feb. 1–Apr. 1	7 "	55 degrees
Celery	Feb. 15–Apr. 1	8 "	50 "
Corn	Apr. 1–May 1	2 "	65 "
Cucumber	Mar. 15–May 1	10 "	75 "
Egg-plant	Mar. 1–Apr. 15	7 "	75 "
Kohlrabi	Mar. 1–Apr. 1	7 "	55 "
Lettuce	Feb. 15–Apr. 1	5 "	55 "
Melon, musk.	Apr. 1–May 1	7 "	75 "
Melon, water	Apr. 1–May 1	7 "	75 "
Okra	Mar. 15–Apr. 15	3 "	65 "
Onion	Jan. 15–Mar. 15	2 "	50 "
Pepper	Mar. 1–Apr. 15	5 "	75 "
Squash	Mar. 15–Apr. 15	7 "	75 "
Tomato	Mar. 1–Apr. 15.	5 "	75 "

The temperatures required by the different varieties will be indicated by the table above. It should be kept as nearly as possible within ten degrees lower and fifteen higher (in the sun) than given. If the nights are still cold, so that the mercury goes near zero, it will be necessary to provide mats or shutters (see illustrations) to cover the glass at night. Or, better still, for the few earliest frames, have double-glass sash, the dead-air space making further protection unnecessary.

VENTILATION: On all days when the temperature within the frame runs up to sixty to eighty degrees, according to variety, give air, either by tilting the sash up at the end or side, and holding in position with a notched stick; or, if the outside temperature permits, strip the glass off altogether.

WATERING: Keep a close watch upon the conditions of the soil, especially if you are using flats instead of planting directly in the soil. Wait until it is fairly dry—never until the plants begin to wilt, however—and then give a thorough soaking, all the soil will absorb. If at all possible do this only in the morning (up to eleven o'clock) on a bright sunny day. Plants in the seedling state are subject to "damping off"—a sudden disease of the stem tissue just at or below the soil, which either kills the seedlings outright, or renders them worthless. Some authorities claim that the degree of moisture or dampness has nothing to do with this trouble. I am not prepared to contradict them, but as far as my own experience goes I am satisfied that the drier the stems and leaves can be kept, so long as the soil is in good condition, the better. I consider this one of the advantages of the "sub-irrigation" method of preparing the seed flats, described above.

TRANSPLANTING: Under this care the little seedlings will come along rapidly. When the second true leaf is forming they will be ready for transplanting or "pricking off," as it is termed in garden parlance. If the plants are at all crowded in the boxes, this should be done just as soon as they are ready, as otherwise they will be injured by crowding and more likely to damp off.

Boxes similar to the seed-flats, but an inch deeper, are provided for transplanting. Fill these with soil as described for frames—sifted through a coarse screen (chicken-wire size) and mixed with one-third rotted manure. Or place an inch of manure, which must be so thoroughly rotted that most of the heat has left, in the bottom, and fill in with soil.

Find or construct a table or bench of convenient height, upon which to work. With a flat piece of stick or one of the types of transplanting forks lift from the seedling box a clump of seedlings, dirt and all, clear to the bottom. Hold this clump in one hand and with the other gently tear away the seedlings, one at a time, discarding all crooked or weak ones. Never attempt to pull the seedlings from the soil in the flats, as the little rootlets are very easily broken off. They should come away almost intact. Water your seed-flats the day previous to transplanting, so that the soil will be in just the right condition, neither wet enough to make the roots sticky nor dry enough to crumble away.

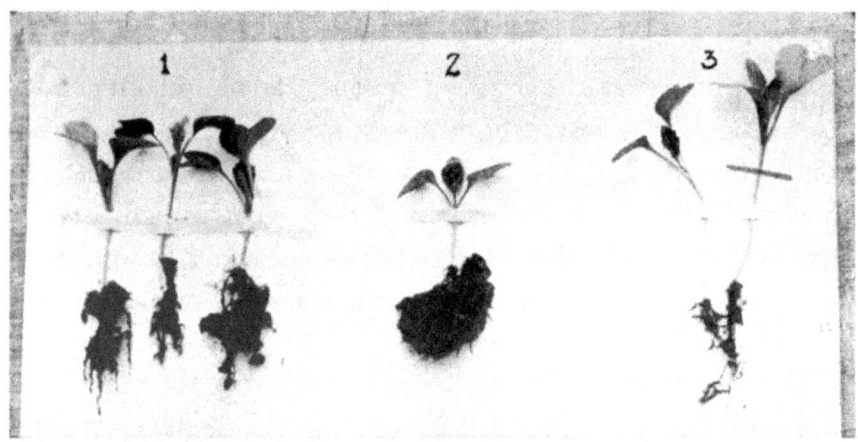

(1) Cabbage seedlings just right for transplanting. (2) Stock seedlings—notice mass of rootlets and adhering earth. (3) Seedlings that were too thickly sown and consequently have become lanky. These should be set in soil as deep as indicated by black line.

The whole story: Grand Rapids lettuce seedlings; in flat ready for setting in frames (or outdoors); and a head ready for the table

Take the little seedling by the stem between thumb and forefinger, and with a small round pointed stick or dibber, or with the forefinger of the other hand, make a hole to receive the roots and about half the length—more if the seedlings are lanky—of the stem. As the seedling drops into place, the tips of both thumbs and forefingers, by one quick, firm movement, compress the earth firmly both down on the roots and against the stem, so that the plant sticks up firmly and may not be readily pulled out. Of course there is a knack about it which cannot be put into words—I could have pricked off a hundred seedlings in the time I am spending in trying to describe the operation, but a little practice will make one reasonably efficient at it.

In my own work this spring, I have applied the "sub-irrigation" idea to this operation also. The manure placed in the bottom of the boxes is thoroughly watered and an inch of soil put in and watered also, and the box then filled and the plants pricked in. By preparing a number of flats at one time, but little additional work is required, and the results have convinced me that the extra trouble is well worthwhile. Of the early cabbage and cauliflower, not two plants in a thousand have dropped out.

Ordinarily about one hundred plants are put in a 13 x 19 inch flat, but if one has room and is growing only a few plants for home use, somewhat better plants may be had if fifty or seventy-five are put in. In either case keep the outside rows close to the edges of the flats, as they will have plenty of room anyway. When the flat is completed, jar the box slightly to level the surface, and give a thorough watering at once, being careful, however, to bend down the plants as little as possible. Set the flats close together on a level surface, and, if the weather is bright, shade from the sun during the middle of the day for two or three days.

From now on keep at the required temperature and water thoroughly on bright mornings as often as the soil in the flats gets on the dry side, as gardeners say—indicated by the whitening and crusting of the surface. Above all, give all the air possible while maintaining the necessary temperature. The quality of the plants will depend more upon this than anything else in the way of care. Whenever the temperature allows, strip off the sash and let the plants have the benefit of the rains. A good rain seems to do them more good than any watering.

Should your plants of cabbage, lettuce, beets or cauliflower by any chance get frozen, do not give them up for lost, for the chances are that the following simple treatment will pull them through: In the first place, shade them thoroughly from the sun; in the second, drench them with cold water, the coldest you can get—if you have to break the ice for it, so much the better. Try, however, to prevent its happening again, as they will be less able to resist subsequent injury.

In hot weather, where watering and ventilation are neglected, the plants will sometimes become infested with the green aphis, which under such conditions multiplies with almost incredible rapidity.

HARDENING OFF: For five days or a week before setting plants in the field they should be thoroughly hardened off. If they have been given plenty of air this treatment will mean little change for them—simply exposing them more each day, until for a few nights they are left entirely without protection. They will then be ready for setting out in the open, an operation which is described in the next chapter.

STARTING PLANTS OUTSIDE

Much of the above is applicable also to the starting of plants out-of-doors, for second and for succession crops, such as celery and late cabbage. Select for the outside seed-bed the most thoroughly pulverized spot to be found, enriched and lightened with fine manure. Mark off rows a foot apart, and to the necessary depth; sow the seed evenly; firm in if the soil is dry, cover lightly with the back of the rake and roll or smooth with the back of the spade, or of a hoe, along the drills. The seed, according to variety, will begin to push through in from four to twenty days. At all times keep the seed-bed clear of weeds; and keep the soil between the rows constantly cultivated. Not unless it is very dry will watering be necessary, but if it is required, give a thorough soaking toward evening.

As the cabbage, celery and similar plants come along it will add to their sturdiness and stockiness to shear off the tops—about half of the large leaves—once or twice after the plants have attained a height of about six inches.

If the precautions concerning seed and soil which I have given are heeded and the details of the work of planting, transplanting and care are carried out, planting time (April) will find the prospective gardener with a supply of good, stocky, healthy plants on hand, and impatient to get them into that carefully prepared garden spot. All of this work has been—or should have been—interesting, but that which follows in the next chapter is more so.

Chapter 9

Sowing and Planting

The importance of having good seeds has already been declared. They must not only grow, but grow into what we have bought them for—be true to name. Without the latter quality we cannot be sure of good gardens, and without the former they will not be full ones. A meagre "stand" from seeds properly sown is a rather exasperating and discouraging experience to encounter. The cost for fertilizing and preparing the land is just as much, and the cost of cultivating very nearly as much, when the rows are full of thrifty plants or strung out with poor ones. Whether you use ten cents' worth or ten dollars' worth, the best seed to be had will be the most economical to buy—to say nothing of the satisfaction that full rows give.

And yet good seedsmen are more thoughtlessly and unjustly abused in the matter of seed vitality than in any other. Inexperienced gardeners seem universally to have the conviction that the only thing required in seed sowing is to cover the seed with soil. What sort of soil it is, or in what condition, or at what depth or temperature the seed is planted, are questions about which they do not trouble themselves to think.

Two conditions—moisture and warmth—are necessary to induce germination of seeds, no matter how full of life they may be; and as was shown in the preceding chapter the different varieties have some choice as to the degree of each, especially of temperature. This means of course that some commonsense must be used in planting, and when planting outdoors, where we cannot regulate the temperature to our need, we simply must regulate our seed sowing to its dictates, no matter how impatient we may be.

To insure the best possible germination, and thus the best gardening, we must, first of all then, settle the question of temperature when sowing out-of-doors. For practical work it serves to divide the garden vegetables into two groups, though in planting, the special suggestions in the following chapter should be consulted.

WHEN TO SOW OUTDOORS

Sow from the end of March to the beginning of May, or when plum and peach trees bloom, the following:

> Beet Cabbage Carrot Cauliflower Celery Endive Kale Kohlrabi Lettuce Onions Parsley Parsnip Peas Radish Spinach Turnip Water-cress

Sow from the beginning of May to the middle of June, or when apple trees bloom, the following:

> Beans Corn Cucumber Melon, musk Melon, water Okra Pumpkin Squash Tomato

Getting the seed to sprout, however, is only the first step in the game; they must be provided with the means of immediately beginning to grow. This means that they should not be left to germinate in loosely packed soil, full of air spaces, ready to dry out at the first opportunity, and to let the tiny seed roots be shriveled up and die.

If the soil is at all dry firm the seed into the rows with the ball of the foot before covering

HOME VEGETABLE GARDENING

Different sorts of drills: (1) single broad drill for large seeds, such as peas or beans; (2) twin drill for same, giving the advantage of more convenient thinning and weeding; (3) "mark" for fine seeds such as lettuce; (4) drill for medium seeds such as beets

The soil should touch the seed—be pressed close about it on all sides, so that the first tiny tap root will issue immediately into congenial surroundings where it can instantly take hold. Such conditions can be found only in a seed-bed fine but light enough to pack, reasonably rich and sufficiently moist, and where, in addition to this, the seed has been properly planted.

METHODS OF PLANTING

The seedbed, as it is called, is the surface prepared to receive the seed, whether for a patch of radishes or an acre of onions. For crops to be sown directly where they are to go, the chapter on Preparation of the Soil takes us to this point, and as stated at the conclusion of that chapter, the final preparation of the bed should be made only immediately prior to its use.

Having, then, good seeds on hand and the soil properly prepared to receive them, the only problem remaining is what way they shall be put in. The different habits of growth characteristic of different plants make it patent at the outset that there must be different methods of planting, for very evidently a cabbage, which occupies but three or four square feet of space and stays in one place to make a head, will not require the same treatment as a winter squash, roaming all over the garden and then escaping under the fence to hide some of its best fruit in the tall grass outside.

The three systems of planting usually employed are known as "drills," "rows" and "hills." I do not remember ever seeing a definition giving the exact distinctions between them; and in horticultural writing they seem to be used, to some extent at least, interchangeably. As a rule "drills" refer to the growing of plants continuously in rows, such as onions, carrots or spinach. "Rows" refer to the growing of plants at fixed distances apart in the rows such as cabbage, or potatoes—the cultivation, except hand weeding and hoeing, being all done in one direction, as with drills. "Hills" refer to the growing of plants usually at equal distances, four feet or more apart each way, with cultivating done in both directions, as with melons and squashes. I describe the different methods at length so that the reader may know more definitely just what is meant by the special instructions given in the following text.

The egg-plant—in the opinion of many the most delicious of all the fruit vegetables

Tomato vines trained against the house, wall or trellis yield fine fruit

SOWING THE SEED

If one observes the suggestions as to temperature just given, and the following precautions in placing the seed within the soil, failure of good seed to germinate is practically impossible. In the first place, plant on a freshly prepared surface, always just before a rain if possible, except in the case of very small seeds, when just after a rain will be better. If the soil is at all dry, or likely to be followed by a spell of hot, dry weather, always firm by using the back of the hoe for small seed, or the ball of the foot for larger ones, such as peas, beans or corn, to press the seed firmly and evenly into the soil before covering. Then when the soil is covered in over the seed, firm along the top of the row very lightly, just enough to mark it and hold the soil in place.

The depth of the drill furrow in which the seed is to be sown will depend (1) on the variety of vegetable, (2) on the season of planting, and (3) on weather conditions. Remember that the seed must be supplied with moisture both to germinate and to continue to exist after germination; and also that it must have soil through which the air can to some extent penetrate. Keeping these things in mind, common sense dictates that seed planted in the spring, or during a wet spell of weather, will not need to be put in as deeply as should the same seed in summer or early autumn, or during a hot, dry spell.

The old general rule is, to cover seed planted under glass, where the moisture can be controlled, to a depth of two or three times its diameter; and out-of-doors, to four or five times. I should say these depths were the minimums desirable. In other words, the smallest seed, such as onion, carrot, lettuce, will go in one-quarter to one-half inch deep. Beets, spinach, parsnips and other medium-sized seed one-half to one inch deep, and peas, beans, corn, etc., two to four inches deep— usually near the first figure.

After the seed is sown it is of course desirable to keep the ground from baking or crusting on top, as it is likely to do after a morning rain followed directly by hot sun. If the seed sprouts have not yet reached the surface of the soil, rake very lightly across the rows with an iron rake;

if they have broken through, work as close as possible to the row. The best implement I have ever seen for this purpose is the disc attachment of the double wheel hoe—see Implements. An ordinarily good garden loam, into which the desirable quantity of short manure has been worked, will give little trouble by raking. In a clay soil, it often will pay, on a small scale, to sift leaf mold, sphagnum moss, or some other light porous covering, over the rows, especially for small seed. The special seed-bed, for starting late cabbage or celery, may easily be sheltered. In very hot, dry weather this method will be a great help.

SETTING OUT PLANTS

The reader has not forgotten, of course, that plants as well as seeds must go into the well managed garden. We have already mentioned the hardening-off process to which they must be subjected before going into the open ground. The flats should also be given a copious watering several hours, or the day before, setting out. All being ready, with your rows made straight and marked off at the correct distances, lift out the plants with a trowel or transplanting fork, and tear or cut them apart with a knife, keeping as much soil as possible with each ball of roots. Distribute them at their positions, but not so many at a time that any will dry out before you get them in place. Get down on your hands and knees, and, straddling the row, proceed to "set." With the left hand, or a trowel or dibber if the ground is not soft, make a hole large enough to take the roots and the better part of the stem, place the plant in position and firm into place by bearing down with the backs of the knuckles, on either side. Proceed so to the end of the row, being careful to keep your toes from undoing your good work behind you, and then finish the job by walking back over the row, still further firming in each plant by pressing down the soil at either side of the stem simultaneously with the balls of the feet. When all the rows are completed, go over the surface with the iron rake, and you will have a job thoroughly done and neatly finished.

HOME VEGETABLE GARDENING

Tomato "tables" result in heavier vines and tomatoes free from rot or blemish

Your garden will be several days earlier for a shelter on the northern exposure

Here they are at last, after all these chapters of planning, preparing and planting

Inviting blight and fruit-rot. For sure results and the best specimens of fruit, always tie tomatoes up

The leaf crops are greatly benefited by early applications of nitrate of soda. Cabbage should grow like this

The fruit crops must have heat and potash. Corn wilts quickly; you must grow your own for the best. Modern large peppers are as mild as apples.

The only satisfactory way to sow seeds—marking, furrowing, dropping, covering and firming, all in one operation, as fast as you can walk. The further advantage of machine sowing—perfectly straight, narrow rows allowing the wheel hoe to shave up close on both sides.

If the weather and soil are exceptionally dry it may be necessary to take the additional precautions, when planting, of putting a pint or so of water in each hole (never on the surface) previous to planting; or of puddling the roots in a thick mixture of rich soil and water. The large leaves also should be trimmed back one-half. In the case of plants that are too tall or succulent, this should be done in any case —better a day or two previous to setting out.

AFTER-CARE

Transplanting should be done whenever possible in dull weather or before rain—or even during it if you really would deserve the name of gardener! If it must be done when the sun continues strong, shade the plants from, say, ten to three o'clock, for a day or two, with half sheets of old newspapers held in tent-shaped position over the plants by stones or earth. If it is necessary to give water, do it toward evening. If the plants have been properly set, however, only extreme circumstances will render this necessary.

Keep a sharp lookout for cut-worms, maggots or other enemies described in Chapter XIII.

And above all, CULTIVATE.

Never let the soil become crusted, even if there is not a weed in sight. Keep the soil loosened up, for that will keep things growing.

Chapter 10

The Cultivation of Vegetables

Before taking up the garden vegetables individually, I shall outline the general practice of cultivation, which applies to all.

The purposes of cultivation are three—to get rid of weeds, and to stimulate growth by

(1) letting air into the soil and freeing unavailable plant food, and
(2) by conserving moisture.

As to weeds, the gardener of any experience need not be told the importance of keeping his crops clean. He has learned from bitter and costly experience the price of letting them get anything resembling a start. He knows that one or two days' growth, after they are well up, followed perhaps by a day or so of rain, may easily double or treble the work of cleaning a patch of onions or carrots, and that where weeds have attained any size they cannot be taken out of sowed crops without doing a great deal of injury. He also realizes, or should, that every day's growth means just so much available plant food stolen from under the very roots of his legitimate crops.

Instead of letting the weeds get away with any plant food, he should be furnishing more, for clean and frequent cultivation will not only break the soil up mechanically, but let in air, moisture and heat—all essential in effecting those chemical changes necessary to convert non- available into available plant food. Long before the science in the case was discovered, the soil cultivators had learned by observation the necessity of keeping the soil nicely loosened about their growing crops. Even the lanky and untutored aborigine saw to it that his squaw not only put a bad fish under the hill of maize but plied her shell hoe over it. Plants need to breathe. Their roots need air. You might as well expect to find the rosy glow of happiness on the wan cheeks of a cotton-mill child slave as to expect to see the luxuriant dark green of healthy plant life in a suffocated garden.

Important as the question of air is, that of water ranks beside it. You may not see at first what the matter of frequent cultivation has to do with water. But let us stop a moment and look into it. Take a strip of blotting paper, dip one end in water, and watch the moisture run up hill, soak up through the blotter. The scientists have labeled that "capillary attraction"—the water crawls up little invisible tubes formed by the texture of the blotter. Now take a similar piece, cut it across, hold the two cut edges firmly together, and try it again. The moisture refuses to cross the line: the connection has been severed.

In the same way the water stored in the soil after a rain begins at once to escape again into the atmosphere. That on the surface evaporates first, and that which has soaked in begins to soak in through the soil to the surface. It is leaving your garden, through the millions of soil tubes, just as surely as if you had a two-inch pipe and a gasoline engine, pumping it into the gutter night and day! Save your garden by stopping the waste. It is the easiest thing in the world to do—cut the pipe in two. And the knife to do it with is— dust. By frequent cultivation of the surface soil—not more than one or two inches deep for most small vegetables—the soil tubes are kept broken, and a mulch of dust is maintained. Try to get over every part of your garden, especially where it is not shaded, once in every ten days or two weeks. Does that seem like too much work? You can push your wheel hoe through, and thus keep the dust mulch as a constant protection, as fast as you can walk. If you wait for the weeds, you will nearly have to crawl through, doing more or less harm by disturbing your growing plants, losing all the plant food (and they will take the cream) which they have consumed, and actually putting in more hours of infinitely more disagreeable work. "A stitch in time saves nine!" Have your thread and needle ready beforehand! If I knew how to give greater emphasis to this subject of thorough cultivation, I should be tempted to devote the rest of this chapter to it. If the beginner at gardening has not been convinced by the facts given, there is only one thing left to convince him—experience.

Having given so much space to the reason for constant care in this matter, the question of methods naturally follows. I want to repeat here, my previous advice—by all means get a wheel hoe. The simplest sorts cost only a few dollars, and will not only save you an infinite amount of time and work, but do the work better, very much better than it can be done by hand. You can grow good vegetables, especially if your garden is a very small one, without one of these labor-savers, but I can assure you that you will never regret the small investment necessary to procure it.

With a wheel hoe, the work of preserving the soil mulch becomes very simple. If one has not a wheel hoe, for small areas very rapid work can be done with the scuffle hoe.

The matter of keeping weeds cleaned out of the rows and between the plants in the rows is not so quickly accomplished. Where hand-work is necessary, let it be done at once. Here are a few practical suggestions that will reduce this work to a minimum,

1. Get at this work while the ground is soft; as soon as the soil begins to dry out after a rain is the best time. Under such conditions the weeds will pull out by the roots, without breaking off.

2. Immediately before weeding, go over the rows with a wheel hoe, cutting shallow, but just as close as possible, leaving a narrow, plainly visible strip which must be hand- weeded.

Lath bean racks provide a largely increased surface exposed to sun and air; they are far better than the old-fashioned poles

When the bean vines cover the frame there is a continuous wall of bearing surface rather than a compact column of it

The best tool for this purpose is the double wheel hoe with disc attachment, or hoes for large plants. (3) See to it that not only the weeds are pulled but that every inch of soil surface is broken up. It is fully as important that the weeds just sprouting be destroyed, as that the larger ones be pulled up. One stroke of the weeder or the fingers will destroy a hundred weed seedlings in less time than one weed can be pulled out after it gets a good start. (4) Use one of the small hand-weeders until you become skilled with it. Not only may more work be done but the fingers will be saved unnecessary wear.

The skillful use of the wheel hoe can be acquired through practice only. The first thing to learn is that it is necessary to watch the wheels only: the blades, disc or rakes will take care of themselves. Other suggestions will be found in the chapter on Implements.

The operation of "hilling" consists in drawing up the soil about the stems of growing plants, usually at the time of second or third hoeing. It used to be the practice to hill everything that could be hilled "up to the eyebrows," but it has gradually been discarded for what is termed "level culture"; and the reader will readily see the reason, from what has been said about the escape of moisture from the surface of the soil; for of course the two upper sides of the hill, which may be represented by an equilateral triangle with one side horizontal, give more exposed surface than the level surface represented by the base. In wet soils or seasons hilling may be advisable, but very seldom otherwise. It has the additional disadvantage of making it difficult to maintain the soil mulch which is so desirable.

ROTATION OF CROPS

There is another thing to be considered in making each vegetable do its best, and that is crop rotation, or the following of any vegetable with a different sort at the next planting.

With some vegetables, such as cabbage, this is almost imperative, and practically all are helped by it. Even onions, which are popularly supposed to be the proving exception to the rule, are healthier, and do as well after some other crop, provided the soil is as finely pulverized and rich as a previous crop of onions would leave it.

Here are the fundamental rules of crop rotation:

1. Crops of the same vegetable, or vegetables of the same family (such as turnips and cabbage) should not follow each other.

2. Vegetables that feed near the surface, like corn, should follow deep-rooting crops.

3. Vines or leaf crops should follow root crops.

4. Quick-growing crops should follow those occupying the land all season.

These are the principles which should determine the rotations to be followed in individual cases. The proper way to attend to this matter is when making the planting plan. You will then have time to do it properly, and will need to give it no further thought for a year.

HOME VEGETABLE GARDENING

Blanching celery in drain tile. Put the tile on a few weeks before the celery is wanted

With the above suggestions in mind, and put to use, it will not be difficult to give the crops mentioned in the following chapter those special attentions which are needed to make them do their very best.

Chapter 11

The Vegetables and Their Special Needs

The garden vegetables may be considered in three groups, in each of which the various varieties are given somewhat similar treatment: the root crops, such as beets and carrots; the leaf crops, such as cabbage and lettuce; the fruit crops, such as melons and tomatoes.

ROOT CROPS

Under the first section we will consider:

Beet Carrot Kohlrabi Leek Onion Parsnip Potato Salsify Turnip

Any of these may be sown in April, in drills (with the exception of potatoes) twelve to eighteen inches apart. The soil must be rich and finely worked, in order that the roots will be even and smooth—in poor or ill-prepared soil they are likely to be misshapen, or "sprangling." They must be thinned out to the proper distances, which should be done if possible on a cloudy day, hand-weeded as often as may be required, and given clean and frequent cultivation. All, with the exception of leeks and potatoes, are given level culture. All will be greatly benefited, when about one-third grown, by a top dressing of nitrate of soda.

Beet:—Beets do best in a rather light soil. Those for earliest use are started under glass (as described previously) and set out six to seven inches apart in rows a foot apart.

The first outdoor sowing is made as soon as the soil is ready in spring, and the seed should be put in thick, as not all will come through if bad weather is encountered. When thinning out, the small plants that are removed, tops and roots cooked together, make delicious greens.

The late crop, for fall and winter use, sow the last part of June. For this crop the larger varieties are used, and on rich soil will need six to eight inches in the row and fifteen inches between rows.

Carrot:—Carrots also like a soil that is rather on the sandy side, and on account of the depth to which the roots go, it should be deep and fine. The quality will be better if the soil is not too rich. A few for extra early use may be grown in the hotbeds or frame. If radishes and carrots are sown together, in alternating rows six inches apart, the former will be used by the time the carrots need the room, and in this way a single 3 x 6 ft. sash will yield a good supply for the home garden. Use Chantenay or Ox-Heart (see Chapter XII) for this purpose.

The late crop is sometimes sown between rows of onions, skipping every third row, during June, and left to mature when the onions are harvested; but unless the ground is exceptionally free from weeds, the plan is not likely to prove successful.

Kohlrabi:—While not truly a "root crop"—the edible portion being a peculiar globular enlargement of the stem—its culture is similar, as it may be sown in drills and thinned out. Frequently, however, it is started in the seed-bed and transplanted, the main crop (for market) being sown in May or June. A few of these from time to time will prove very acceptable for the home table. They should be used when quite young; as small as two inches being the tenderest.

Leek:—To attain its best the leek should be started in the seed-bed, late in April, and transplanted in late June, to the richest, heaviest soil available. Hill up from time to time to blanch lower part of stalk; or a few choice specimens may be had by fitting cardboard collars around the stem and drawing the earth up to these, not touching the stalk with earth.

Onions:—Onions for use in the green state are grown from white "sets," put out early in April, three to four inches apart in rows twelve inches apart; or from seed sown the previous fall and protected with rough manure during the winter. These will be succeeded by the crop from "prickers" or seedlings started under glass in January or February. As onions are not transplanted before going to the garden, sow directly in the soil rather than in flats. It is safest to cover the bed with one-half inch to one inch of coarse sand, and sow the seed in this. To get stocky plants trim back twice, taking off the upper half of leaves each time, and trim back the roots one-half to two- thirds at the time of setting out, which may be any time after the middle of April. These in turn will be succeeded by onions coming from the crop sown from seed in the open.

The above is for onions eaten raw in the green state when less than half grown. For the main crop for bulbs, the home supply is best grown from prickers as described above. Prize-taker and Gibraltar are mostly used for this purpose, growing to the size of the large Spanish onions sold at grocery stores. For onions to be kept for late winter and spring use, grow from seed, sowing outdoors as early as possible.

No vegetable needs a richer or more perfectly prepared soil than the onion; and especial care must be taken never to let the weeds get a start. They are gathered after the tops dry down and wither, when they should be pulled, put in broad rows for several days in the sun, and then spread out flat, not more than four inches deep, under cover with plenty of light and air. Before severe freezing store in slatted barrels, as described in Chapter XIV.

Try to get over every part of your garden, especially where it is not shaded, once in every ten days to break up the surface crust; the plants will show the result

HOME VEGETABLE GARDENING

With beans the ground may be worked over more deeply than with some of the other vegetables. Hoe the earth up about them a little each time. Do not touch when foliage is wet

Parsnip:—Sow as early as possible, in deep rich soil, but where no water will stand during fall and winter. The seed germinates very slowly, so the seed-bed should be very finely prepared. They will be ready for use in the fall, but are much better after the first frosts. For method of keeping see Chapter XIV.

Potato:—If your garden is a small one, buy your main supply of potatoes from some nearby farmer, first trying half a bushel or so to be sure of the quality. Purchase in late September or October when the crop is being dug and the price is low.

For an extra early and choice supply for the home garden, start a peck or so in early March, as follows: Select an early variety, seed of good size and clean; cut to pieces containing one or two eyes, and pack closely together on end in flats of coarse sand. Give these full light and heat, and by the middle to end of April they will have formed dense masses of roots, and nice, strong, stocky sprouts, well leaved out. Dig out furrows two and a half feet apart, and incorporate well-rotted manure in the bottom, with the soil covering this until the furrow is left two to three inches deep. Set the sprouted tubers, pressing firmly into the soil, about twelve inches apart, and cover in, leaving them thus three to four inches below the surface. Keep well cultivated, give a light top dressing of nitrate of soda—and surprise all your neighbors! This system has not yet come extensively into use, but is practically certain of producing excellent results.

For the main crop, if you have room, cut good seed to one or two eyes, leaving as much of the tuber as possible to each piece, and plant thirteen inches apart in rows three feet apart. Cultivate deeply until the plants are eight to ten inches high and then shallow but frequently. As the vines begin to spread, hill up moderately, making a broad, low ridge. Handle potato-bugs and blight as directed in Chapter XIII. For harvesting see Chapter XIV.

While big crops may be grown on heavy soils, the quality will be very much better on sandy, well drained soils. Planting on well-rotted sod, or after green manuring, such as clover or rye, will also improve the looks and quality of the crop. Like onions, they need a high percentage of potash in manures or fertilizers used; this may be given in sulphate of potash. Avoid planting on ground enriched with fresh barnyard manure or immediately after a dressing of lime.

Salsify:—The "vegetable oyster," or salsify, is to my taste the most delicious root vegetable grown. It is handled practically in the same way as the parsnip, but needs, if possible, ground even more carefully prepared, in order to keep the main root from sprangling. If a fine light soil cannot be had for planting, it will pay to hoe or hand-plow furrows where the drills are to be—not many will be needed, and put in specially prepared soil, in which the seed may get a good start.

Radish:—To be of good crisp quality, it is essential with radishes to grow them just as quickly as possible. The soil should be rather sandy and not rich in fresh manure or other nitrogenous fertilizers, as this tends to produce an undesirable amount of leaves at the expense of the root. If the ground is at all dry give a thorough wetting after planting, which may be on the surface, as the seeds germinate so quickly that they will be up before the soil has time to crust over. Gypsum or land-plaster, sown on white and worked into the soil, will improve both crop and quality. They are easily raised under glass, in autumn or spring in frames, requiring only forty to fifty degrees at night. It is well to plant in the hotbed, after a crop of lettuce. Or sow as a double crop, as suggested under Carrots. For outside crops, sow every ten days or two weeks.

Turnip:—While turnips will thrive well on almost any soil, the quality —which is somewhat questionable at the best—will be much better on sandy or even gravelly soil. Avoid fresh manures as much as possible, as the turnip is especially susceptible to scab and worms. They are best when quite small and for the home table a succession of sowing, only a few at a time, will give the best results.

LEAF CROPS

Under leaf crops are considered also those of which the stalk or the flower heads form the edible portion, such as celery and cauliflower.

> Asparagus Brussels Sprouts Cabbage Cauliflower Celery Endive Kale Lettuce Parsley Rhubarb Spinach

The quality of all these will depend largely upon growing them rapidly and without check from the seed-bed to the table. They are all great nitrogen-consumers and therefore take kindly to liberal supplies of yard manure, which is high in nitrogen. For celery the manure is best applied to some preceding crop, such as early cabbage. The others will take it "straight." Most of these plants are best started under glass or in the seed-bed and transplanted later to permanent positions. They will all be helped greatly by a top-dressing of nitrate of soda, worked into the soil as soon as they have become established. This, if it fails to produce the dark green healthy growth characteristic of its presence, should be followed by a second application after two or three weeks—care being taken, of course, to use it with reason and restraint, as directed in Chapter VI.

Another method of growing good cabbages and similar plants, where the ground is not sufficiently rich to carry the crop through, is to "manure in the hill," either yard or some concentrated manure being used. If yard manure, incorporate a good forkful with the soil where each plant is to go. (If any considerable number are being set, it will of course be covered in a furrow—first being trampled down, with the plow). Another way, sure of producing results, and not inconvenient for a few hundred plants, is to mark out the piece, dig out with a spade or hoe a hole some five inches deep at each mark, dilute poultry manure in an old pail until about the consistency of thick mud, and put a little less than half a trowelful in each hole. Mix with the soil and cover, marking the spot with the back of the hoe, and then set the plants. By this method, followed by a top-dressing of nitrate of soda, I have repeatedly grown fine cabbage, cauliflower, lettuce and sprouts. Cotton-seed meal is also very valuable for manuring in the hill—about a handful to a plant, as it is rich in nitrogen and rapidly decomposes.

The cabbage group is sometimes hilled up, but if set well down and frequently cultivated, on most soils this will not be necessary. They all do best in very deep, moderately heavy soil, heavily manured and rather moist. An application of lime some time before planting will be a beneficial precaution. With this group rotation also is almost imperative.

The most troublesome enemies attacking these plants are: the flea-beetle, the cabbage-worm, the cabbage-maggot (root) and "club-root"; directions for fighting all of which will be found in the following chapter.

Asparagus:—Asparagus is rightly esteemed one of the very best spring vegetables. There is a general misconception, however—due to the old methods of growing it—concerning the difficulty of having a home supply. As now cared for, it is one of the easiest of all vegetables to grow, when once the beds are set and brought to bearing condition. Nor is it difficult to make the bed, and the only reason why asparagus is not more universally found in the home garden, beside that mentioned above, is because one has to wait a year for results.

In selecting a spot for the asparagus bed, pick out the earliest and best drained soil available, even if quite sandy it will do well. Plow or dig out trenches three feet apart and sixteen to twenty inches deep. In the bottoms of these tramp down firmly six to eight inches of old, thoroughly rotted manure. Cover with six to eight inches of good soil— not that coming from the bottom of the trench—and on this set the crowns or root-clumps—preferably one-year ones—being careful to spread the roots out evenly, and covering with enough soil to hold in position, making them firm in the soil. The roots are set one foot apart. Then fill in level, thus leaving the crowns four to six inches below the surface. As the stalks appear give a light dressing of nitrate of soda and keep the crop cleanly cultivated. (Lettuce, beets, beans or any of the small garden vegetables may be grown between the asparagus rows during the first part of the season, for the first two years, thus getting some immediate return from labor and manure). The stalks should not be cut until the second spring after planting and then only very lightly. After that full crops may be had.

After the first season, besides keeping cleanly cultivated at all times, in the fall clear off and burn all tops and weeds and apply a good coating of manure. Dig or lightly cultivate this in the spring, applying also a dressing of nitrate of soda, as soon as the stalks appear. If the yield is not heavy, give a dressing of bone or of the basic fertilizers mentioned earlier. It is not difficult to grow plants from seed, but is generally more satisfactory to get the roots from some reliable seedsman.

Broccoli:-The broccoli makes a flower head as does the cauliflower. It is, however, inferior in quality and is not grown to any extent where the latter will succeed. It has the one advantage of being hardier and thus can be grown where the cauliflower is too uncertain to make its culture worthwhile. For culture directions see Cauliflower.

Brussels Sprouts:—In my opinion this vegetable leaves the cabbage almost as far behind as the cauliflower does. It is, if anything, more easily grown than cabbage, except that the young plants do not seem able to stand quite so much cold. When mature, however, it seems to stand almost any amount of freezing, and it is greatly improved by a few smart frosts, although it is very good when succeeding the spring crop of cauliflower. It takes longer to mature than either cabbage or cauliflower.

Cabbage:—Cabbage is one of the few vegetables which may be had in almost as good quality from the green-grocer as it can be grown at home, and as it takes up considerable space, it may often be advisable to omit the late sorts from the home garden if space is very limited. The early supply, however, should come from the garden—some people think it should stay there, but I do not agree with them. Properly cooked it is a very delicious vegetable.

What has already been said covers largely the conditions for successful culture. The soil should be of the richest and deepest, and well dressed with lime.

Lettuce is grown with advantage between the rows of early cabbage, and after both are harvested the ground is used for celery. The early varieties may be set as closely as eighteen inches in the row, and twenty-four between rows. The lettuce is taken out before the row is needed.

The late crop is started in the outside seed-bed about June 1st to 15th. It will help give better plants to cut back the tops once or twice during growth, and an occasional good soaking in dry weather will prove very beneficial. They are set in the field during July, and as it often is very dry at this time, those extra precautions mentioned in directions for setting out plants, in the preceding chapter, should be taken. If the newly set plants are dusted with wood ashes, it will be a wise precaution against insect pests.

Cauliflower:—The cauliflower is easily the queen of the cabbage group: also it is the most difficult to raise. (1) It is the most tender and should not be set out quite so early. (2) It is even a ranker feeder than the cabbage, and just before heading up will be greatly improved by applications of liquid manure. (3) It must have water, and unless the soil is a naturally damp one, irrigation, either by turning the hose on between the rows, or directly around the plants, must be given—two or three times should be sufficient. (4) The heads must be protected from the sun. This is accomplished by tying up the points of leaves, so as to form a tent, or breaking them (snap the mid- rib only), and folding them down over the flower. (5) They must be used as soon as ready, for they deteriorate very quickly. Take them while the head is still solid and firm, before the little flower tips begin to open out.

Sow seeds for succession crops in a frame, where you can water them and keep close watch

The plants all ready to be set out in the open garden. Remember above all to set them in *firmly*

Celery:—This is another favorite vegetable which has a bad reputation to live down. They used to plant it at the bottom of a twelve-inch trench and spend all kinds of unnecessary labor over it. It can be grown perfectly well on the level and in the average home garden.

As to soil, celery prefers a moist one, but it must be well drained. The home supply can, however, be grown in the ordinary garden, especially if water may be had in case of injurious drouth.

For the early crop the best sorts are the White Plume and Golden Self- blanching. Seed is sown in the last part of February or first part of March. The seed is very fine and the greatest pains must be taken to give the best possible treatment. The seed should be pressed into the soil and barely covered with very light soil—half sifted leaf-mold or moss. Never let the boxes dry out, and as soon as the third or fourth leaf comes, transplant; cut back the outside leaves, and set as deeply as possible without covering the crown. The roots also, if long, should be cut back. This trimming of leaves and roots should be given at each transplanting, thus assuring a short stocky growth.

Culture of the early crop, after setting out, is easier than that for the winter crop. There are two systems:

1. The plants are set in rows three or four feet apart, six inches in the row, and blanched, either by drawing up the earth in a hill and working it in about the stalks with the fingers (this operation is termed "handling"), or else by the use of boards laid on edge along the rows, on either side.

2. The other method is called the "new celery culture," and in it the plants are set in beds eight inches apart each way (ten or twelve inches for large varieties), the idea being to make the tops of the plants supply the shade for the blanching. This method has two disadvantages: it requires extra heavy manuring and preparation of soil, and plenty of moisture; and even with this aid the stalks never attain the size of those grown in rows. The early crop

should be ready in August. The quality is never so good as that of the later crops.

A mushroom bed coming into bearing. Notice the solidity of the buttons and shortness of stems—both good qualities

For the main or winter crop, sow the seed about April 1st. The same extra care must be taken as in sowing under glass. In hot, dry weather, shade the beds; never let them dry out. Transplant to second bed as soon as large enough to develop root system, before setting in the permanent position. When setting in late June or July, be sure to put the plants in up to the hearts, not over, and set firmly. Give level clean culture until about August 15th, when, with the hoe, wheel hoe or cultivator, earth should be drawn up along the rows, followed by "handling." The plants for early use are trenched (see Chapter XIV), but that left for late use must be banked up, which is done by making the hills higher still, by the use of the spade. For further treatment see Chapter XIV. Care must be taken not to perform any work in the celery patch while the plants are wet.

Corn salad or Fetticus:—This salad plant is not largely grown. It is planted about the middle of April and given the same treatment as spinach.

Chicory:—This also is little grown. The Witloof, a kind now being used, is however much more desirable. Sow in drills, thin to five or six inches, and in August or September, earth up, as with early celery, to blanch the stalks, which are used for salads, or boiled. Cut-back roots, planted in boxes of sand placed in a moderately warm dark place and watered, send up a growth of tender leaves, making a fine salad.

Chervil:—Curled chervil is grown the same as parsley and used for garnishing or seasoning. The root variety resembles the stump-rooted carrot, the quality being improved by frost. Sow in April or September. Treat like parsnip.

Chives:—Leaves are used for imparting an onion flavor. A clump of roots set put will last many years.

Cress:—Another salad little grown in the home garden. To many, however, its spicy, pungent flavor is particularly pleasing. It is easily grown, but should be planted frequently—about every two weeks. Sow in drills, twelve to fourteen inches apart. Its only special requirement is moisture. Water is not necessary, but if a bed can be started in some clean stream or pool, it will take care of itself. Upland cress or "pepper grass" grows in ordinary garden soil, being one of the very first salads. Sow in April, in drills twelve or fourteen inches apart. It grows so rapidly that it may be had in five or six weeks. Sow frequently for succession, as it runs to seed very quickly.

Chard:—See Spinach.

Dandelion:—This is an excellent "greens," but as the crop is not ready until second season from planting it is not grown as much as it should be. Sow the seed in April—very shallow. It is well to put in with it a few lettuce or turnip seed to mark the rows. Drills should be one foot apart, and plants thinned to eight to twelve inches. The quality is infinitely superior to the wild dandelion and may be still further improved by blanching. If one is content to take a small crop, a cutting may be made in the fall, the same season as the sowing.

Endive:—This salad vegetable is best for fall use. Sow in June or July, in drills eighteen to twenty-four inches apart, and thin to ten to twelve inches. To be fit for use it must be blanched, either by tying up with raffia in a loose bunch, or by placing two wide boards in an inverted V shape over the rows; and in either case be sure the leaves are dry when doing this.

Kale:—Kale is a non-heading member of the cabbage group, used as greens, both in spring and winter. It is improved by frost, but even then is a little tough and heavy. Its chief merit lies in the fact that it is easily had when greens of the better sorts are hard to get, as it may be left out and cut as needed during winter—even from under snow. The fall crop is given the same treatment as late cabbage. Siberian kale is sown in September and wintered-over like spinach.

Lettuce:—Lettuce is grown in larger quantities than all the other salad plants put together. By the use of hotbeds it may be had practically the year round. The first sowing for the spring under-glass crop is made in January or February. These are handled as for the planting outside—see Chapter VIII.—but are set in the frames six to eight inches each way, according to variety. Ventilate freely during the day when over 55° give 45° at night. Water only when needed, but then thoroughly, and preferably only on mornings of bright sunny days.

The plants for first outdoor crops are handled as already described. After April 1st planting should be made every two weeks. During July and August the seed-beds must be kept shaded and moist. In August, first sowing for fall under-glass crop is made, which can be matured in coldframes; later sowings going into hotbeds.

Early Jersey Wakefield, the standard sugar-loaf cabbage, fine in quality

Drumhead Savoy cabbage. The Savoy type is the finest in quality of all the cabbages

Early Snowball cauliflower. Not quite so hardy as cabbage. To keep white, tie leaves over maturing heads

Kohlrabi, Early White and Early Purple (Vienna) which should be used while still small and tender

In quality, I consider the hard-heading varieties superior to the loose-heading sorts, but of course that is a matter of taste. The former is best for crops maturing from the middle of June until September, the latter for early and late sowings, as they mature more quickly. The cos type is good for summer growing but should be tied up to blanch well. To be at its best, lettuce should be grown very rapidly, and the use of top-dressings of nitrate are particularly beneficial with this crop. The ground should be light, warm, and very rich, and cultivation shallow but frequent.

Mushroom:—While the mushroom is not a garden crop, strictly speaking, still it is one of the most delicious of all vegetables for the home table, and though space does not permit a long description of the several details of its culture, I shall try to include all the essential points as succinctly as possible, (1) The place for the bed may be found in any sheltered, dry spot—cellar, shed or greenhouse— where an even temperature of 53 to 58 degrees can be maintained and direct sunlight excluded. (Complete darkness is not necessary; it is frequently so considered, but only because in dark places the temperature and moisture are apt to remain more even.) (2) The material is fresh horse-manure, from which the roughest of the straw has been shaken out. This is stacked in a compact pile and trampled—wetting down if at all dry—to induce fermentation. This process must be repeated four or five times, care being required never to let the heap dry out and burn; time for re-stacking being indicated by the heap's steaming. At the second or third turning, add about one-fifth, in bulk, of light loam. (3) When the heat of the pile no longer rises above 100 to 125 degrees (as indicated by a thermometer) put into the beds, tramping or beating very firmly, until about ten inches deep. When the temperature recedes to 90 degrees, put in the spawn. Each brick will make a dozen or so pieces. Put these in three inches deep, and twelve by nine inches apart, covering lightly. Then beat down the surface evenly. After eight days, cover with two inches of light loam, firmly compacted. This may be covered with a layer of straw or other light material to help maintain an even degree of moisture, but should be removed as soon as the mushrooms begin to appear. Water only when the soil is very dry; better if water is warmed to about 60 degrees. When gathering never leave stems in the bed as they are likely to breed maggots. The crop should appear in six to eight weeks after spawning the bed.

Parsley:—This very easily grown little plant should have at least a row or two in the seed-bed devoted to it. For use during winter, a box or a few pots may be filled with cut-back roots and given moderate temperature and moisture. If no frames are on hand, the plants usually will do well in a sunny window.

Parsley seed is particularly slow in germinating. Use a few seeds of turnip or carrot to indicate the rows, and have the bed very finely prepared.

Rhubarb:—This is another of the standard vegetables which no home garden should be without. For the bed pick out a spot where the roots can stay without interfering with the plowing and working of the garden—next the asparagus bed, if in a good early location, will be as good as any. One short row will supply a large family. The bed is set either with roots or young plants, the former being the usual method. The ground should first be made as deep and rich as possible. If poor, dig out the rows, which should be four or five feet apart, to a depth of two feet or more and work in a foot of good manure, refilling with the best of the soil excavated. Set the roots about four feet apart in the row, the crowns being about four inches below the surface. No stalks should be cut the first season; after that they will bear abundantly many years.

In starting from seed, sow in March in frames or outside in April; when well along-about the first of June—set out in rows, eighteen by twelve inches. By the following April they will be ready for their permanent position.

Manuring in the fall, as with asparagus, to be worked in in the spring, is necessary for good results. I know of no crop which so quickly responds to liberal dressings of nitrate of soda, applied first just as growth starts in in the spring. The seed stalks should be broken off as fast as they appear, until late in the season.

Sea-Kale:—When better known in this country, sea-kale will be given a place beside the asparagus and rhubarb, for, like them, it may be used year after year. Many believe it superior in quality to either asparagus or cauliflower.

It is grown from either seed or pieces of the root, the former method, being probably the more satisfactory. Sow in April, in drills fourteen inches apart, thinning to five or six. Transplant in the following spring as described for rhubarb—but setting three feet apart each way. In the fall, after the leaves have fallen—and every succeeding fall— cover each crown with a shovelful of clean sand and then about eighteen inches of earth, dug out from between the rows. This is to blanch the spring growth. After cutting, shovel off the earth and sand and enrich with manure for the following season's growth.

Spinach:—For the first spring crop of this good and wholesome vegetable, the seed is sown in September, and carried over with a protection of hay or other rough litter. Crops for summer and fall are sown in successive plantings from April on, Long-Standing being the best sort to sow after about May 15th. Seed of the New Zealand spinach should be soaked several hours in hot water, before being planted.

For the home garden, I believe that the Swiss chard beet is destined to be more popular, as it becomes known, than any of the spinaches. It is sown in plantings from April on, but will yield leaves all season long; they are cut close to the soil, and in an almost incredibly short time the roots have thrown up a new crop, the amount taken during the season being wonderful.

Spinach wants a strong and very rich soil, and dressings of nitrate show good results.

THE FRUIT CROPS

Under this heading are included:

Bean, dwarf Bean, pole Corn Peas Cucumber Egg-plant Melon, musk Melon, water Okra Pepper Pumpkins Squash Tomato

Most of these vegetables differ from both the preceding groups in two important ways. First of all, the soil should not be made too rich, especially in nitrogenous manures, such as strong fresh yard-manure; although light dressings of nitrate of soda are often of great help in giving them a quick start—as when setting out in the field. Second, they are warm-weather loving plants, and nothing is gained by attempting to sow or set out the plants until all danger from late frosts is over, and the ground is well warmed up. (Peas, of course, are an exception to this rule, and to some extent the early beans.) Third, they require much more room and are grown for the most part in hills.

Light, warm, "quick," sandy to gravelly soils, and old, fine, well rotted manure—applied generally in the hill besides that plowed under, make the best combination for results. Such special hills are prepared by marking off, digging out the soil to the depth of eight to ten inches, and eighteen inches to two feet square, and incorporating several forkfuls of the compost. A little guano, or better still cottonseed meal, say 1/2 to 1 gill of the former, or a gill of the latter, mixed with the compost when putting into the hill, will also be very good. Hills to be planted early should be raised an inch or two above the surface, unless they are upon sloping ground.

The greatest difficulty in raising all the vine fruits—melons, etc.— is in successfully combating their insect enemies—the striped beetle, the borer and the flat, black "stink-bug," being the worst of these. Remedies will be suggested in the next chapter. But for the home garden, where only a few hills of each will be required, by far the easiest and the only sure way of fighting them will be by protecting with bottomless boxes, large enough to cover the hills, and covered with mosquito netting, or better, "plant-protecting cloth," which has the additional merit of giving the hills an early start. These boxes may be easily made of one-half by eight-inch boards, or from ordinary cracker-boxes, such as used for making flats. Plants so protected in the earlier stages of growth will usually either not be attacked, or will, with the assistance of the remedies described in the following chapter, be able to withstand the insect's visits.

Beans, dwarf:—Beans are one of the most widely liked of all garden vegetables—and one of the most easily grown. They are very particular about only one thing—not to have a heavy wet soil. The dwarf or bush sorts are planted in double or single drills, eighteen to twenty-four inches apart, and for the first sowing not much over an inch deep. Later plantings should go in two to three inches deep, according to soil. Ashes or some good mixed fertilizer high in potash, applied and well mixed in at time of planting, will be very useful.

As the plants gain size they should be slightly hilled—to help hold the stalks up firmly. Never work over or pick from the plants while they are wet. The dwarf limas should not be planted until ten to fourteen days later than the early sorts. Be sure to put them in edgeways, with the eye down, and when there is no prospect of immediate rain, or the whole planting is fairly sure to be lost.

Beans, pole:—The pole varieties should not go in until about the time for the limas. Plant in specially prepared hills (see above) ten to twenty seeds, and when well up thin, leaving three to five. Poles are best set when preparing the hills. A great improvement over the old-fashioned pole is made by nailing building laths firmly across 2 x 3-in. posts seven or eight feet high (see illustration). To secure extra early pods on the poles pinch back the vines at five feet high.

Corn:—For extra early ears, corn may easily be started on sod, as directed for cucumbers. Be sure, however, not to get into the open until danger from frost is over—usually at least ten days after it is safe for the first planting, which is seldom made before May 1st. Frequent, shallow cultivation is a prime necessity in growing this crop. When well up, thin to four stalks to a hill—usually five to seven kernels being planted. A slight hilling when the tassels appear will be advisable. Plant frequently for succession crops. The last sowing may be made as late as the first part of July if the seed is well firmed in, to assure immediate germination. Sweet corn for the garden is frequently planted in drills, about three feet apart, and thinning to ten to twelve inches.

Cucumber:—This universal favorite is easily grown if the striped beetle is held at bay. For the earliest fruits start on sod in the frames: Cut out sods four to six inches square, where the grass indicates rich soil. Pack close together in the frame, grass side down, and push seven or eight seeds into each, firmly enough to be held in place, covering with about one and a half inches of light soil; water thoroughly and protect with glass or cloth, taking care to ventilate, as described in Chapter VIII. Set out in prepared hills after danger of frost is over.

Outside crop is planted directly in the hills, using a dozen or more seeds and thinning to three or four.

Egg-plant:—The egg-plant is always started under glass, for the Northern States, and should be twice transplanted, the second time into pots, to be of the best size when put out. This should not be until after tomatoes are set, as it is perhaps the tenderest of all garden vegetables as regards heat. The soil should be very rich and as moist as can be selected. If dry, irrigating will be necessary. This should not be delayed until the growth becomes stunted, as sudden growth then induced is likely to cause the fruit to crack.

Watch for potato-bugs on your egg-plants. They seem to draw these troublesome beetles as a magnet does iron filings, and I have seen plants practically ruined by them in one day. As they seem to know there will not be time to eat the whole fruit they take pains to eat into the stems. The only sure remedy is to knock them off with a piece of shingle into a pan of water and kerosene. Egg-plants are easily burned by Paris green, and that standard remedy cannot be so effectively used as on other crops; hellebore or arsenate of lead is good. As the season of growth is very limited, it is advisable, besides having the plants as well developed as possible when set out, to give a quick start with cotton-seed meal or nitrate, and liquid manure later is useful, as they are gross feeders. The fruits are ready to eat from the size of a turkey egg to complete development.

Melon, musk:—The culture of this delicious vegetable is almost identical with that of the cucumber. If anything it is more particular about having light soil. If put in soil at all heavy, at the time of preparing the hill, add sand and leaf-mold to the compost, the hills made at least three feet square, and slightly raised. This method is also of use in planting the other vine crops.

Melon, water:—In the warm Southern States watermelons may be grown cheaply, and they are so readily shipped that in the small home gardens it will not pay to grow them, for they take up more space than any other vegetable, with the exception of winter squash. The one advantage of growing them, where there is room, is that better quality than that usually to be bought may be obtained. Give them the hottest spot in the garden and a sandy quick soil. Use a variety recommended for your particular climate. Give the same culture as for musk melon, except that the hill should be at least six to ten feet apart each way. By planting near the edge of the garden, and pinching back the vines, room may be saved and the ripening up of the crop made more certain.

Okra:—Although the okra makes a very strong plant—and incidentally is one of the most ornamental of all garden vegetables— the seed is quickly rotted by wet or cold. Sow not earlier than May 25th, in warm soil, planting thinly in drills, about one and a half inches deep, and thinning to a foot or so; cultivate as with corn in drills. All pods not used for soup or stems during summer may be dried and used in winter.

Peas:—With care in making successive sowings, peas may be had during a long season. The earliest, smooth varieties are planted in drills twelve to eighteen inches apart, early in April. These are, however, of very inferior quality compared to the wrinkled sorts, which may now be had practically as early as the others. With the market gardener, the difference of a few days in the maturing of the crop is of a great deal more importance than the quality, but for the home garden the opposite is true.

Another method of planting the dwarf-growing kinds is to make beds of four rows, six to eight inches apart, with a two-foot alley between beds. The tall-growing sorts must be supported by brush or in other ways; and are put about four feet apart in double rows, six inches apart. The early varieties if sown in August will usually mature a good fall crop. The early plantings should be made in light, dry soil and but one inch deep; the later ones in deep loam. In neither case should the ground be made too rich, especially in nitrogen; and it should not be wet when the seed is planted.

Pepper:—A dozen pepper plants will give abundance of pods for the average family. The varieties have been greatly improved within recent years in the quality of mildness.

The culture recommended for egg-plant is applicable also to the pepper. The main difference is that, although the pepper is very tender when young, the crop maturing in the autumn will not be injured by considerable frost.

Pumpkin:—The "sugar" or "pie" varieties of the pumpkin are the only ones used in garden culture, and these only where there is plenty of ground for all other purposes. The culture is the same as that for late squashes, which follows.

Squash:—For the earliest squash the bush varieties of Scallop are used; to be followed by the summer Crookneck and other summer varieties, best among which are the Fordhook and Delicata. For all, hills should be prepared as described at the beginning of this section and in addition it is well to mix with manure a shovelful of coal ashes, used to keep away the borer, to the attack of which the squash is particularly liable. The cultivation is the same as that used for melons or cucumbers, except that the hills for the winter sorts must be at least eight feet apart and they are often put twelve.

Tomato:—For the earliest crop, tomatoes are started about March 1st. They should be twice transplanted, and for best results the second transplanting should be put into pots—or into the frames, setting six to eight inches each way. They are not set out until danger of frost is over, and the ground should not be too rich; old manure used in the hill, with a dressing of nitrate at setting out, or a few days after, will give them a good start. According to variety, they are set three to five feet apart—four feet, where staking or trellising is given, as it should always be in garden culture, will be as much as the largest- growing plants require. It will pay well, both for quality and quantity of fruit, to keep most of the suckers cut or rubbed off. The ripening of a few fruits may be hastened by tying paper bags over the bunches, or by picking and ripening on a board in the hot sun. For ripening fruit after frost see Chapter XIV.

A sharp watch should be kept for the large green tomato-worm, which is almost exactly the color of the foliage. His presence may first be noticed by fruit and leaves eaten. Hand-picking is the best remedy. Protection must be made against the cutworm in localities where he works.

All the above, of course, will be considered in connection with the tabulated information as to dates, depths and distances for sowing, quantities, etc., given in the table in Chapter IV, and is supplemented by the information about insects, diseases and harvesting given in Chapters XIII and XIV, and especially in the Chapter on Varieties which follows, and which is given separately from the present chapter in order that the reader may the more readily make out a list, when planning his garden or making up his order sheet for the seedsman.

Chapter 12

Best Varieties of the Vegetable Garden

It is my purpose in this chapter to assist the gardener of limited experience to select varieties sure to give satisfaction.

To the man or woman planning a garden for the first time there is no one thing more confusing than the selection of the best varieties. This in spite of the fact that catalogues should be, and might be, a great help instead of almost an actual hindrance.

I suppose that seedsmen consider extravagance in catalogues, both in material and language, necessary, or they would not go to the limit in expense for printing and mailing, as they do. But from the point of view of the gardener, and especially of the beginner, it is to be regretted that we cannot have the plain unvarnished truth about varieties, for surely the good ones are good enough to use up all the legitimate adjectives upon which seedsmen would care to pay postage. But such is not the case. Every season sees the introduction of literally hundreds of new varieties—or, as is more often the case, old varieties under new names—which have actually no excuse for being unloaded upon the public except that they will give a larger profit to the seller. Of course, in a way, it is the fault of the public for paying the fancy prices asked—that is, that part of the public which does not know. Commercial planters and experienced gardeners stick to well-known sorts. New varieties are tried, if at all, by the packet only—and then "on suspicion."

In practically every instance the varieties mentioned have been grown by the author, but his recommendations are by no means based upon personal experience alone. Wherever introductions of recent years have proved to be actual improvements upon older varieties, they are given in preference to the old, which are, of course, naturally much better known.

It is impossible for any person to pick out this, that or the other variety of a vegetable and label it unconditionally "the best." But the person who wants to save time in making out his seed list can depend upon the following to have been widely tested, and to have "made good."

Asparagus:—While there are enthusiastic claims put forth for several of the different varieties of asparagus, as far as I have seen any authentic record of tests (Bulletin 173, N. J. Agr. Exp. Station), the prize goes to Palmetto, which gave twenty-eight per cent. more than its nearest rival, Donald's Elmira. Big yield alone is frequently no recommendation of a vegetable to the home gardener, but in this instance it does make a big difference; first, because Palmetto is equal to any other asparagus in quality, and second, because the asparagus bed is producing only a few weeks during the gardening season, and where ground is limited, as in most home gardens, it is important to cut this waste space down as much as possible. This is for beds kept in good shape and highly fed. Barr's Mammoth will probably prove more satisfactory if the bed is apt to be more or less neglected, for the reason that under such circumstances it will make thicker stalks than the Palmetto.

Beans (dwarf):—Of the dwarf beans there are three general types: the early round-podded "string" beans, the stringless round- pods, and the usually more flattish "wax" beans. For first early, the old reliable Extra Early Red Valentine remains as good as any sort I have ever tried. In good strains of this variety the pods have very slight strings, and they are very fleshy. It makes only a small bush and is fairly productive and of good quality. The care-taking planter, however, will put in only enough of these first early beans to last a week or ten days, as the later sorts are more prolific and of better quality. Burpee's Stringless Greenpod is a good second early. It is larger, finer, stringless even when mature, and of exceptionally handsome appearance. Improved Refugee is the most prolific of the green-pods, and the best of them for quality, but with slight strings. Of the "wax" type, Brittle Wax is the earliest, and also a tremendous yielder. The long-time favorite, Rust-proof Golden Wax, is another fine sort, and an especially strong healthy grower. The top-notch in quality among all bush beans is reached, perhaps, in Burpee's White Wax—the white referring not to the pods, which are of a light yellow, and flat —but to the beans, which are pure white in all stages of growth. It has one unusual and extremely valuable quality—the pods remain tender longer than those of any other sort.

Of the dwarf limas there is a new variety which is destined, I think, to become the leader of the half-dozen other good sorts to be had. That is the Burpee Improved. The name is rather misleading, as it is not an improved strain of the Dreer's or Kumerle bush lima, but a mutation, now thoroughly fixed. The bushes are stronger-growing and much larger than those of the older types, reaching a height of nearly three feet, standing strongly erect; both pods and beans are much larger, and it is a week earlier. Henderson's new Early Giant I have not yet tried, but from the description I should say it is the same type as the above. Of the pole limas, the new Giant-podded is the hardiest—an important point in limas, which are a little delicate in constitution anyway, especially in the seedling stage—and the biggest yielder of any I have grown and just as good in quality—and there is no vegetable much better than well-cooked limas. With me, also, it has proved as early as that old standard, Early Leviathan, but this may have been a chance occurrence. Ford's Mammoth is another excellent pole lima of large size. Of the other pole beans, the two that are still my favorites are Kentucky Wonder, or Old Homestead, and Golden Cluster. The former has fat meaty green pods, entirely stringless until nearly mature, and of enormous length. I have measured many over eight and a half inches long—and they are borne in great profusion. Golden Cluster is one of the handsomest beans I know. It is happily named, for the pods, of a beautiful rich golden yellow color, hang in generous clusters and great profusion. In quality it has no superior; it has always been a great favorite with my customers. One need never fear having too many of these, as the dried beans are pure white and splendid for winter use. Last season I tried a new pole bean called Burger's Green-pod Stringless or White-seeded Kentucky Wonder (the dried seeds of the old sort being brown). It did well, but was in so dry a place that I could not tell whether it was an improvement over the standard or not. It is claimed to be earlier.

Beets:—In beets, varieties are almost endless, but I confess that I have found no visible difference in many cases. Edmund's Early and Early Model are good for first crops. The Egyptian strains, though largely used for market, have never been as good in quality with me. For the main crop I like Crimson Globe. In time it is a second early, of remarkably good form, smooth skin and fine quality and color.

Broccoli:—This vegetable is a poorer cousin of the cauliflower (which, by the way, has been termed "only a cabbage with a college education"). It is of little use where cauliflower can be grown, but serves as a substitute in northern sections, as it is more hardy than that vegetable. Early White French is the standard sort.

Brussels sprouts:—This vegetable, in my opinion, is altogether too little grown. It is as easy to grow as fall and winter cabbage, and while the yield is less, the quality is so much superior that for the home garden it certainly should be a favorite. Today (Jan. 19th) we had for dinner sprouts from a few old plants that had been left in transplanting boxes in an open coldframe. These had been out all winter—with no protection, repeatedly freezing and thawing, and, while of course small, they were better in quality than any cabbage you ever ate. Dalkeith is the best dwarf-growing sort. Danish Prize is a new sort, giving a much heavier yield than the older types. I have tried it only one year, but should say it will become the standard variety.

Cabbage:—In cabbages, too, there is an endless mix-up of varieties. The Jersey Wakefield still remains the standard early. But it is at the best but a few days ahead of the flat-headed early sorts which stand much longer without breaking, so that for the home garden a very few heads will do. Glory of Enkhuisen is a new early sort that has become a great favorite. Early Summer and Succession are good to follow these, and Danish Ballhead is the best quality winter cabbage, and unsurpassed for keeping qualities. But for the home garden the Savoy type is, to my mind, far and away the best. It is not in the same class with the ordinary sorts at all. Perfection Drumhead Savoy is the best variety. Of the red cabbages, Mammoth Rock is the standard.

Carrots:—The carrots are more restricted as to number of varieties. Golden Ball is the earliest of them all, but also the smallest yielder. Early Scarlet Horn is the standard early, being a better yielder than the above. The Danvers Half-long is probably grown more than all other kinds together. It grows to a length of about six inches, a very attractive deep orange in color. Where the garden soil is not in excellent condition, and thoroughly fined and pulverized as it should be, the shorter-growing kinds, Ox-heart and Chantenay, will give better satisfaction. If there is any choice in quality, I should award it to Chantenay.

Cauliflower;—There is hardly a seed catalogue which does not contain its own special brand of the very best and earliest cauliflower ever introduced. These are for the most part selected strains of either the old favorite, Henderson's Snowball, or the old Early Dwarf Erfurt. Snowball, and Burpee's Best Early, which resembles it, are the best varieties I have ever grown for spring or autumn. They are more likely to head, and of much finer quality than any of the large late sorts. Where climatic conditions are not favorable to growing cauliflower, and in dry sections, Dry-weather is the most certain to form heads.

Celery:—For the home garden the dwarf-growing, "self-blanching" varieties of celery are much to be preferred. White Plume and Golden Self-blanching are the best. The former is the earliest celery and of excellent quality, but not a good keeper. Recent introductions in celery have proved very real improvements. Perhaps the best of the newer sorts, for home use, is Winter Queen, as it is more readily handled than some of the standard market sorts. In quality it has no superior. When put away for winter properly, it will keep through April.

Corn:—You will have to suit yourself about corn. I have not the temerity to name any best varieties—every seedsman has about half a dozen that are absolutely unequaled. For home use, I have cut my list down to three: Golden Bantam, a dwarf-growing early of extraordinary hardiness—can be planted earlier than any other sort and, while the ears are small and with yellow kernels, it is exceptionally sweet and fine in flavor. This novelty of a few years since, has attained wide popular favor as quickly as any vegetable I know. Seymour's Sweet Orange is a new variety, somewhat similar to Golden Bantam, but later and larger, of equally fine quality. White Evergreen, a perfected strain of Stowell's Evergreen, a standard favorite for years, is the third. It stays tender longer than any other sweet corn I have ever grown.

Cucumbers:—Of cucumbers also there is a long and varied list of names. The old Extra Early White Spine is still the best early; for the main crop, some "perfected" form of White Spine. I myself like the Fordhood Famous, as it is the healthiest strain I ever grew, and has very large fruit that stays green, while being of fine quality. In the last few years the Davis Perfect has won great popularity, and deservedly so. Many seedsmen predict that this is destined to become the leading standard—and where seedsmen agree let us prick up our ears! It has done very well with me, the fruit being the handsomest of any I have grown. If it proves as strong a grower it will replace Fordhood Famous with me.

Sow kale for use in fall and winter when greens are scarce. Frost only improves it

Seedlings of Prizetaker onions, started in compost covered with one inch of sand. The large onions are from previous year's crop, started in the same way. They were prize-takers at several local fairs

Cos lettuce has more flavor than the old sorts of regular head-lettuce. Paris White is a good variety

French Argenteuil asparagus—a new variety that has won favor everywhere. This bunch of twelve stalks weighed three pounds

Egg-plant:—New York Improved Purple is still the standard, but it has been to a large extent replaced by Black Beauty, which has the merit of being ten days earlier and a more handsome fruit. When once tried it will very likely be the only sort grown.

Endive:—This is a substitute for lettuce for which I personally have never cared. It is largely used commercially. Broad-leaved Batavian is a good variety. Giant Fringed is the largest.

Kale:—Kale is a foreigner which has never been very popular in this country. Dwarf Scott Curled is the tenderest and most delicate (or least coarse) in flavor.

Kohlrabi:—This peculiar mongrel should be better known. It looks as though a turnip had started to climb into the cabbage class and stopped half-way. When gathered young, not more than an inch and a half in diameter at the most, they are quite nice and tender. They are of the easiest cultivation. White Vienna is the best.

Leek:—For those who like this sort of thing it is—just the sort of thing they like. American Flag is the best variety, but why it was given the first part of that name, I do not know.

Lettuce:—To cover the lettuces thoroughly would take a chapter by itself. For lack of space, I shall have to mention only a few varieties, although there are many others as good and suited to different purposes. For quality, I put Mignonette at the top of the list, but it makes very small heads. Grand Rapids is the best loose- head sort—fine for under glass, in frames and early outdoors. Last fall from a bench 40 x 4 ft., I sold $36 worth in one crop, besides some used at home. I could not sell winter head lettuce to customers who had once had this sort, so good was its quality. May King and Big Boston are the best outdoor spring and early summer sorts. New York and Deacon are the best solid cabbage-head types for resisting summer heat, and long standing. Of the cos type Paris White is good.

Muskmelon:—The varieties of muskmelon are also without limit. I mention but two—which have given good satisfaction out of a large number tried, in my own experience. Netted Gem (known as Rocky Ford) for a green-fleshed type, and Emerald Gem for salmon-fleshed. There are a number of newer varieties, such as Hoodoo, Miller's Cream, Montreal, Nutmeg, etc., all of excellent quality.

Watermelon:—With me (in Connecticut) the seasons are a little short for this fruit. Cole's Early and Sweetheart have made the best showing. Halbert Honey is the best for quality.

Okra:—In cool sections the Perfected Perkins does best, but it is not quite so good in quality as the southern favorite, White Velvet. The flowers and plants of this vegetable are very ornamental.

Defender is one of the best colored-flesh mid-season varieties

Eden Gem is a favorite variety of the green-flesh sorts

Muskmelons of this sort—Mary variety—are susceptible to disease

Banquet is a comparatively small, round, mid-season melon

Osage is good for late crop

The Superior is a good late muskmelon of the green-flesh variety

Onion:—For some unknown reason, different seedsmen call the same onion by the same name. I have never found any explanation of this, except that a good many onions given different names in the catalogues are really the same thing. At least they grade into each other more than other vegetables. With me Prizetaker is the only sort now grown in quantity, as I have found it to outyield all other yellows, and to be a good keeper. It is a little milder in quality than the American yellows—Danvers and Southport Globe. When started under glass and transplanted out in April, it attains the size and the quality of the large Spanish onions of which it is a descendant. Weathersfield Red is the standard flat red, but not quite so good in quality or for keeping as Southport Red Globe. Of the whites I like best Mammoth Silver-skin. It is ready early and the finest in quality, to my taste, of all the onions, but not a good keeper. Ailsa Craig, a new English sort now listed in several American catalogues, is the best to grow for extra fancy onions, especially for exhibiting; it should be started in February or March under glass.

Parsley:—Emerald is a large-growing, beautifully colored and mild-flavored sort, well worthy of adoption.

Parsnip:—This vegetable is especially valuable because it may be had at perfection when other vegetables are scarce. Hollow Crown ("Improved," of course!) is the best.

Peas:—Peas are worse than corn. You will find enough exclamation points in the pea sections of catalogues to train the vines on. If you want to escape brain-fag and still have as good as the best, if not better, plant Gradus (or Prosperity) for early and second early; Boston Unrivaled (an improved form of Telephone) for main crop, and Gradus for autumn. These two peas are good yielders, free growers and of really wonderfully fine quality. They need bushing, but I have never found a variety of decent quality that does not.

Pepper:—Ruby King is the standard, large, red, mild pepper, and as good as any. Chinese Giant is a newer sort, larger but later. The flesh is extremely thick and mild. On account of this quality, it will have a wider range of use than the older sorts.

Pumpkins:—The old Large Cheese, and the newer Quaker Pie, are as prolific, hardy and fine in quality and sweetness as any.

Potato:—Bovee is a good early garden sort, but without the best of culture is very small. Irish Cobbler is a good early white. Green Mountain is a universal favorite for main crop in the East—a sure yielder and heavy-crop potato of excellent quality. Uncle Sam is the best quality potato I ever grew. Baked, they taste almost as rich as chestnuts.

Radish:—I do not care to say much about radishes; I do not like them. They are, however, universal favorites. They come round, half-long, long and tapering; white, red, white-tipped, crimson, rose, yellow-brown and black; and from the size of a button to over a foot long by fifteen inches in circumference—the latter being the new Chinese or Celestial. So you can imagine what a revel of varieties the seedsmen may indulge in. I have tried many—and cut my own list down to two, Rapid-red (probably an improvement of the old standard, Scarlet Button), and Crimson Globe (or Giant), a big, rapid, healthy grower of good quality, and one that does not get "corky." A little land-plaster, or gypsum, worked into the soil at time of planting, will add to both appearance and quality in radishes.

Spinach:—The best variety of spinach is Swiss Chard Beet (see below). If you want the real sort, use Long Season, which will give you cuttings long after other sorts have run to seed. New Zealand will stand more heat than any other sort. Victoria is a newer variety, for which the claim of best quality is made. In my own trial I could not notice very much difference. It has, however, thicker and "savoyed" leaves.

Salsify:—This is, to my taste, the most delicious of all root vegetables. It will not do well in soil not deep and finely pulverized, but a row or two for home use can be had by digging and fining before sowing the seed. It is worth extra work. Mammoth Sandwich is the best variety.

Squash:—Of this fine vegetable there are no better sorts for the home garden than the little Delicata, and Fordhook. Vegetable Marrow is a fine English sort that does well in almost all localities. The best of the newer large-vined sorts is The Delicious. It is of finer quality than the well known Hubbard. For earliest use, try a few plants of White or Yellow Bush Scalloped. They are not so good in quality as either Delicata or Fordhook, which are ready within a week or so later. The latter are also excellent keepers and can be had, by starting plants early and by careful storing, almost from June to June.

HOME VEGETABLE GARDENING

Mammoth Sandwich Island salsify, the vegetable oyster, is a delicious root vegetable

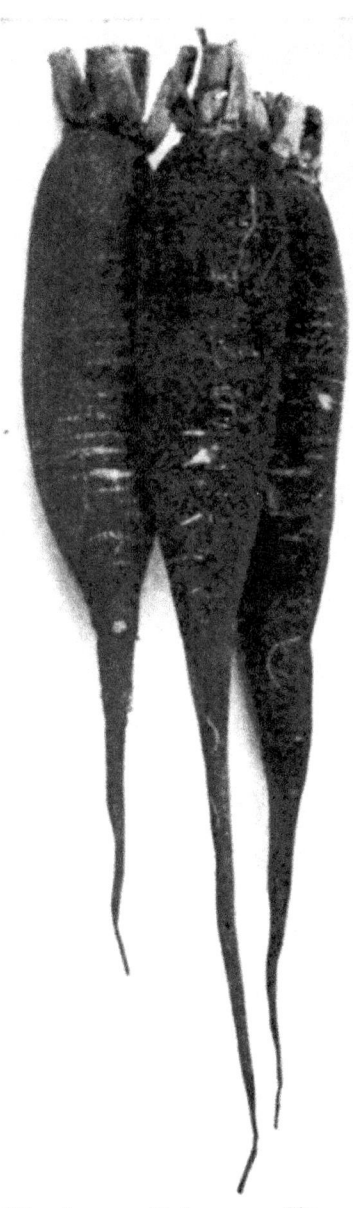

Black radishes. They come also in red, white, scarlet, yellow and combination colors

Tomato:—If you have a really hated enemy, give him a dozen seed catalogues and ask him to select for you the best four tomatoes. But unless you want to become criminally involved, send his doctor around the next morning. A few years ago I tried over forty kinds. A good many have been introduced since, some of which I have tried.

I am prepared to make the following statements: Earliana is the earliest quality tomato, for light warm soils, that I have ever grown; Chalk's Jewel, the earliest for heavier soils (Bonny Best Early resembles it); Matchless is a splendid main-crop sort; Ponderosa is the biggest and best quality—but it likes to split. There is one more sort, which I have tried one year only, so do not accept my opinion as conclusive. It is the result of a cross between Ponderosa and Dwarf Champion—one of the strongest-growing sorts. It is called Dwarf Giant. The fruits are tremendous in size and in quality unsurpassed by any. The vine is very healthy, strong and stocky. I believe this new tomato will become the standard main crop for the home garden. By all means try it. And that is a good deal to say for a novelty in its second year!

Turnip:—The earliest turnip of good quality is the White Milan. There are several others of the white-fleshed sorts, but I have never found them equal in quality for table to the yellow sorts. Of these, Golden Ball (or Orange Jelly) is the best quality. Petrowski is a different and distinct sort, of very early maturity and of especially fine quality. If you have room for but one sort in your home garden, plant this for early, and a month later for main crop.

Do not fail to try some of this year's novelties. Half the fun of gardening is in the experimenting. But when you are testing out the new things in comparison with the old, just take a few plants of the latter and give them the same extra care and attention.

Very often the reputation of a novelty is built upon the fact that in growing it on trial the gardener has given it unusual care and the best soil and location at his command. Be fair to the standards—and very often they will surprise you fully as much as the novelties.

Chapter 13

Insects, Diseases and How to Fight Them

I use the term "methods of fighting" rather than the more usual one, "remedies," because by both experience and study I am more and more convinced that so long as the commercial fields of agriculture remain in the present absolutely unorganized condition, and so long as the gardener—home or otherwise—who cares to be neglectful and thus become a breeder of all sorts of plant pests, is allowed so to do—just so long we can achieve no remedy worth the name. When speaking of a remedy in this connection we very frequently are putting the cart before the horse, and refer to some means of prevention. Prevention is not only the best, but often the only cure. This the gardener should always remember.

This subject of plant enemies has not yet received the attention from scientific investigators which other branches of horticulture have, and it is altogether somewhat complicated.

Before taking up the various insects and diseases the following analysis and list will enable the reader to get a general comprehension of the whole matter.

Plant enemies are of two kinds—

(1) insects, and
(2) diseases.

The former are of two kinds,

(a) insects which chew or eat the leaves or fruit;
(b) insects which suck the juices therefrom.

The diseases also are of two kinds—

(a) those which result from the attack of some fungus, or germ;
(b) those which attack the whole organism of the plant and are termed "constitutional."

Concerning these latter practically nothing is known.

It will be seen at once, of course, that the remedy to be used must depend upon the nature of the enemy to be fought. We can therefore reduce the matter to a simple classification, as follows:

PLANT ENEMIES

Insects	Class
Eating	a
Sucking	b

Diseases	
Parasitical	c
Constitutional	d

It will be of some assistance, particularly as regards quick reference, to give the following table, which shows at a glance the method of fighting any enemy, the presence of which is known or anticipated.

REMEDIES

Mechanical — Number
- Covered boxes 1
- Collars 2
- Cards 3

Destructive
- Hand-picking 4
- Kerosene emulsion 5
- Whale-oil soap 6
- Miscible oils 7
- Tobacco dust 8
- Carbolic acid emulsion 9
- Corrosive sublimate 10
- Bordeaux mixture 11

Poisonous
- Paris green 12
- Arsenate of lead 13
- Hellebore 14

While this may seem quite a formidable list, in practice many of these pests will not appear, and under ordinary circumstances the following six remedies out of those mentioned will suffice to keep them all in check, if used in time: Covered boxes, hand-picking, kerosene emulsion, tobacco dust, Bordeaux mixture, arsenate of lead.

However, that the home gardener may be prepared to meet any contingency, I shall take up in brief detail the plant enemies mentioned and the remedies suggested.

Aphis:—The small, soft green plant-lice. They seldom attack healthy growing plants in the field, but are hard to keep off under glass. If once established it will take several applications to get rid of them.

Use kerosene or soap emulsion, or tobacco dust. There are also several trade-marked preparations that are good. Aphine, which may be had of any seed house, has proved very effective in my own work, and it is the pleasantest to use that I have so far found.

Enemy	Attacking	Class	Remedy
Aphis (Plant-lice).	Cabbage and other plants, especially under glass.	b	5, 8, 6
Asparagus-beetle..	Asparagus.	a	13, 12
Asparagus rust ...	Asparagus.	c	11
Black-rot.	Cabbage and the cabbage group..	d	10
Borers.	Squash.	b	4
Caterpillars	Cabbage group.	a	12, 14, 4
Caterpillars	Tomato.	a	4
Club-root	Cabbage group.	c	(page 163)
Cucumber-beetle (Striped beetle)	Cucumber and vines.	a	1, 11, 8
Cucumber-wilt ...	Cucumber and vines.	c	11
Cucumber-blight..	Cucumber, muskmelon, cabbage..	c	11
Cut-worm.	Cabbage, tomato, onion.	a	2, 4, 12, 13
Flea-beetle.	Potato, turnip, radish.	a	11, 5
Potato-beetle.	Potato and egg-plant.	a	12, 13, 4
Potato-blight.	Potato.	c	11
Potato-scab	Potato (tubers).	c	10
Root-maggot.	Radish, onion, cabbage, melons..	a	4, 3, 9
Squash-bug	Squash, pumpkin.	b	4, 8, 12. 5
White-fly	Plants; cucumber, tomato.	b	6, 5, 8
White-grub	Plants.	a	4

Asparagus-beetle:—This pest will give little trouble on cleanly cultivated patches. Thorough work with arsenate of lead (1 to 25) will take care of it.

Black-rot:—This affects the cabbage group, preventing heading, by falling of the leaves. In clean, thoroughly limed soil, with proper rotations, it is not likely to appear. The seed may be soaked, in cases where the disease has appeared previously, for fifteen minutes in a pint of water in which one of the corrosive sublimate tablets which are sold at drug stores is dissolved.

Borers:—This borer is a flattish, white grub, which penetrates the main stem of squash or other vines near the ground and seems to sap the strength of the plant, even when the vines have attained a length of ten feet or more. His presence is first made evident by the wilting of the leaves during the noonday heat. Coal ashes mixed with the manure in the hill, is claimed to be a preventative. Another is to plant some early squash between the hills prepared for the winter crop, and not to plant the latter until as late as possible. The early squash vines, which act as a trap, are pulled and burned. Last season almost half the vines in one of my pieces were attacked after many of the squashes were large enough to eat. With a little practice I was able to locate the borer's exact position, shown by a spot in the stalk where the flesh was soft, and of a slightly different color. With a thin, sharp knife-blade the vines were carefully slit lengthwise on this spot, the borer extracted and killed and the vines in almost every instance speedily recovered. Another method is to root the vines by heaping moist earth over several of the leaf joints, when the vines have attained sufficient length.

Cabbage-caterpillar:—This small green worm, which hatches upon the leaves and in the forming heads of cabbage and other vegetables of the cabbage group, comes from the eggs laid by the common white or yellow butterfly of early spring. Pick off all that are visible, and spray with kerosene emulsion if the heads have not begun to form. If they have, use hellebore instead. The caterpillar or worm of tomatoes is a large green voracious one. Hand-picking is the only remedy.

Club-root:—This is a parasitical disease attacking the cabbage group, especially in ground where these crops succeed each other. Lime both soil and seed-bed—at least the fall before planting, unless using a special agricultural lime. The crop infested is sometimes carried through by giving a special dressing of nitrate of soda, guano or other quick-acting powerful fertilizer, and hilled high with moist earth, thus giving a special stimulation and encouraging the formation of new roots. While this does not in any way cure the disease, it helps the crop to withstand its attack. When planting again be sure to use crop rotation and to set plants not grown in infested soil.

Cucumber-beetle:—This is the small, black-and-yellow-striped beetle which attacks cucumbers and other vines and, as it multiplies rapidly and does a great deal of damage before the results show, they must be attended to immediately upon appearance. The vine should be protected with screens until they crowd the frames, which should be put in place before the beetles put in an appearance. If the beetles are still in evidence when the vines get so large that the screens must be removed, keep sprayed with Bordeaux mixture. Plaster, or fine ashes, sifted on the vines will also keep them off to some extent, by keeping the leaves covered.

Cucumber-wilt:—This condition accompanies the presence of the striped beetle, although supposed not to be directly caused by it. The only remedy is to get rid of the beetles as above, and to collect and burn every wilted leaf or plant.

Cucumber-blight or Mildew is similar to that which attacks muskmelons, the leaves turning yellow, dying in spots and finally drying up altogether. Where there is reason to fear an attack of this disease, or upon the first appearance, spray thoroughly with Bordeaux, 5-5-50, and repeat every ten days or so. The spraying seems to be more effective on cucumbers than on melons.

Cut-worm:—The cut-worm is perhaps the most annoying of all garden pests. Others do more damage, but none is so exasperating. He works at night, attacks the strongest, healthiest plants, and is content simply to cut them off, seldom, apparently, eating much or carrying away any of the severed leaves or stems, although occasionally I have found such bits, especially small onion tops, dragged off and partly into the soil. In small gardens the quickest and best remedy is hand-picking. As the worms work at night they may be found with a lantern; or very early in the morning. In daytime by digging about in the soil wherever a cut is found, and by careful search, they can almost invariably be turned out. As a preventive, and a supplement to hand-picking, a poisoned bait should be used. This is made by mixing bran with water until a "mash" is made, to which is added a dusting of Paris green or arsenate of lead, sprayed on thickly and thoroughly worked through the mass. This is distributed in small amounts—a tablespoonful or so to a place along the row or near each hill or plant—just as they are coming up or set out. Still another method, where only a few plants are put out, is to protect each by a collar of tin or tar paper.

Flea-beetle:—This small, black or striped hard-shelled mite attacks potatoes and young cabbage, radish and turnip plants. It is controlled by spraying with kerosene emulsion or Bordeaux.

Potato-beetle:—The striped Colorado beetle, which invariably finds the potato patch, no matter how small or isolated. Paris green, dry or sprayed, is the standard remedy. Arsenate of lead is now largely used. On small plots hand-picking of old bugs and destruction of eggs (which are laid on under side of leaves) is quick and sure.

Potato-blight:—Both early and late forms of blight are prevented by Bordeaux, 5-5-50, sprayed every two weeks. Begin early— when plants are about six inches high.

Potato-scab:—Plant on new ground; soak the seed in solution prepared as directed under No. 10, which see; allow no treated tubers to touch bags, boxes, bins or soil where untreated ones have been kept.

Root-maggot:—This is a small white grub, often causing serious injury to radishes, onions and the cabbage group. Liming the soil and rotation are the best preventives. Destroy all infested plants, being sure to get the maggots when pulling them up. The remaining plants should be treated with a gill of strong caustic lime water, or solution of muriate of potash poured about the root of each plant, first removing an inch or so of earth. In place of these solutions carbolic acid emulsion is sometimes used; or eight to ten drops of bisulphide of carbon are dropped into a hole made near the roots with the dibber and then covered in. Extra stimulation, as directed for Club-root, will help carry the plants through.

Squash-bug:—This is the large, black, flat "stink-bug," so destructive of squash and the other running vines. Protection with frames, or hand-picking, are the best home garden remedies. The old bugs may be trapped under boards and by early vines. The young bugs, or "sap-sucking nymphs," are the ones that do the real damage. Heavy tobacco dusting, or kerosene emulsion will kill them.

White-Fly:—This is the most troublesome under glass, where it is controlled by fumigation, but occasionally is troublesome on plants and tomato and cucumber vines. The young are scab-like insects and do the real damage. Spray with kerosene emulsion or whale-oil soap.

White-grub or muck-worm:—When lawns are infested the sod must be taken up, the grubs destroyed and new sward made. When the roots of single plants are attacked, dig out, destroy the grubs and, if the plant is not too much injured, reset.

The remedies given in the table above are prepared as follows:

MECHANICAL REMEDIES

1. Covered boxes:—These are usually made of half-inch stuff, about eight inches high and covered with mosquito netting, wire or "protecting cloth"—the latter having the extra advantage of holding warmth overnight.

2. Collars are made of old cans with the bottoms removed, cardboard or tarred paper, large enough to go over the plant and an inch or so into the ground.

3. Cards are cut and fitted close around the stem and for an inch or so upon the ground around it, to prevent maggots going down the stem to the root. Not much used.

DESTRUCTIVE REMEDIES

1. Hand-picking is usually very effective, and if performed as follows, not very disagreeable: Fasten a small tin can securely to a wooden handle and fill one-third full of water and kerosene; make a small wooden paddle, with one straight edge and a rather sharp point; by using this in the right hand and the pan in the left, the bugs may be quickly knocked off. Be sure to destroy all eggs when hand-picking is used.

2. Kerosene emulsion is used in varying strengths; for method of preparing, see Chapter XVII.

3. For use of whale-oil soap and miscible oils, see Chapter XVII.

4. Tobacco dust:—This article varies greatly. Most sorts are next to worthless, but a few of the brands especially prepared for this work (and sold usually at $3 per hundred pounds, which will last two ordinary home gardens a whole season) are very convenient to use, and effective. Apply with a duster, like that described in Implements.

5. Carbolic acid emulsion:—1 pint crude acid, 1 lb. soap and 1 gal. water. Dissolve the soap in hot water, add balance of water and pump into an emulsion, as described for kerosene emulsion.

6. Corrosive sublimate is used to destroy scab on potatoes for seed by dissolving 1 oz. in 7 gals, of water. The same result is obtained by soaking for thirty minutes in a solution of commercial formalin, at the rate of 1 gill to 15 gals. of water.

7. Bordeaux mixture:—See Chapter XVII.

POISONOUS REMEDIES

1. Paris green:—This is the standard remedy for eating-bugs and worms. With a modern dusting machine it can be put on dry, early in the morning when the dew is still on. Sometimes it is mixed with plaster. For tender plants easily burned by the pure powder, and where dusting is not convenient, it is mixed with water at the rate of 1 lb. to 50 to 100 gals. and used as a spray. In mixing, make a paste of equal quantities of the powder and quicklime, and then mix thoroughly in the water. It must be kept stirred up when using.

2. Arsenate of lead:—This has two advantages over Paris green: It will not burn the foliage and it will stay on several times as long. Use from 4 to 10 lbs. in 100 gals. of water; mix well and strain before putting in sprayer. See also Chapter XVII.

3. Hellebore:—A dry, white powder, used in place of Nos. 12 or 13 on vegetables or fruit that is soon to be eaten. For dusting, use 1 lb. hellebore to 5 of plaster or flour. For watering or spraying, at rate of 1 lb. to 12 gals. of water.

PRECAUTIONS

So much for what we can do in actual hand-to-hand, or rather hand-to-mouth, conflict with the enemy. Very few remedies have ever proved entirely successful, especially on crops covering any considerable area. It will be far better, far easier and far more effective to use the following means of precaution against plant pest ravages: First, aim to have soil, food and plants that will produce a rapid, robust growth without check. Such plants are seldom attacked by any plant disease, and the foliage does not seem to be so tempting to eating- insects; besides which, of course, the plants are much better able to withstand their attack if they do come. Second, give clean, frequent culture and keep the soil busy. Do not have old weeds and refuse lying around for insects and eggs to be sheltered by. Burn all leaves, stems and other refuse from plants that have been diseased. Do not let the ground lie idle, but by continuous cropping keep the bugs, caterpillars and eggs constantly rooted out and exposed to their natural enemies. Third, practice crop rotation. This is of special importance where any root disease is developed. Fourth, watch closely and constantly for the first appearance of trouble. The old adages "eternal vigilance is the price of peace," and "a stitch in time saves nine," are nowhere more applicable than to this matter. And last, and of extreme importance, be prepared to act at once. Do not give the enemy an hour's rest after his presence is discovered. In almost every case it is only by having time to multiply, that damage amounting to anything will be done.

If you will keep on hand, ready for instant use, a good hand-sprayer and a modern powder gun, a few covered boxes, tobacco dust, arsenate of lead and materials for kerosene emulsion and Bordeaux mixture, and are not afraid to resort to hand-picking when necessary, you will be able to cope with all the plant enemies you are likely to encounter. The slight expense necessary—considering that the two implements mentioned will last for years with a little care—will pay as handsome a dividend as any garden investment you can make.

Chapter 14

Harvesting and Storing

It is a very common thing to allow the garden vegetables not used to rot on the ground, or in it. There is a great deal of unnecessary waste in this respect, for a great many of the things so neglected may just as well be carried into winter, and will pay a very handsome dividend for the slight trouble of gathering and storing them.

A good frost-proof, cool cellar is the best and most convenient place in which to store the surplus product of the home garden. But, lacking this, a room partitioned off in the furnace cellar and well ventilated, or a small empty room, preferably on the north side of the house, that can be kept below forty degrees most of the time, will serve excellently. Or, some of the most bulky vegetables, such as cabbage and the root crops, may be stored in a prepared pit made in the garden itself.

As it is essential that such a pit be properly constructed, I shall describe one with sufficient detail to enable the home gardener readily to construct it. Select a spot where water will not stand. Put the vegetables in a triangular-shaped pile, the base three or four feet wide, and as long as required. Separate the different vegetables in this pile by stakes about two feet higher than the top of the pile, and label them. Then cover with a layer of clean straw or bog hay, and over this four inches of soil, dug up three feet back from the edges of the pile. This work must be done late in the fall, as nearly as one can judge just before lasting freezing begins, and preferably on a cold morning when the ground is just beginning to freeze; the object being to freeze the partly earth covering at once, so that it will not be washed or blown off. The vegetables must be perfectly dry when stored; dig them a week or so previous and keep them in an airy shed. As soon as this first layer of earth is partly frozen, but before it freezes through, put on another thick layer of straw or hay and cover with twelve inches of earth, keeping the pile as steep as possible; a slightly clayey soil, that may be beaten down firmly into shape with a spade, being best. The pile should be made where it will be sheltered from the sun as much as possible, such as on the north side of a building. The disadvantage of the plan is, of course, that the vegetables cannot be got at until the pile is opened up, in early spring, or late if desired. Its two advantages are that the vegetables stored will be kept in better condition than in any cellar, and that cellar or house room will be saved.

For storing small quantities of the roots, such as carrots or beets, they are usually packed in boxes or barrels and covered in with clean sand. Where an upstairs room has to be used, swamp or sphagnum moss may replace the sand. It makes an ideal packing medium, as it is much lighter and cleaner than the sand. In many localities it may be had for the gathering; in others one may get it from a florist.

In storing vegetables of any kind, and by whatever method, see to it that:

1. They are always clean, dry and sound. The smallest spot or bruise is a danger center, which may spread destruction to the lot.

2. That the temperature, whatever required—in most cases 33-38 degrees being best—is kept as even as possible.

3. That the storage place is kept clean, dry (by ventilation when needed) and sweet (by use of whitewash and lime).

4. That no rats or other rodents are playing havoc with your treasures while you never suspect it.

So many of the vegetables can be kept, for either part or all of the winter, that I shall take them up in order, with brief directions. Many, such as green beans, rhubarb, tomatoes, etc., which cannot be kept in the ordinary ways, may be easily and cheaply canned, and where one has a good cellar, it will certainly pay to get a canning outfit and make use of this method.

Beans:—Almost all the string and snap beans, when dried in the pods, are excellent for cooking. And any pods which have not been gathered in the green state should be picked, as soon as dry (as wet weather is likely to mold or sprout them), and stored in a dry place, or spread on a bench in the sun. They will keep, either shelled or in the dry pods, for winter.

Beets:—In October, before the first hard frosts, take up and store in a cool cellar, in clean, perfectly dry sand, or in pits outside (see Cabbage); do not cut off the long tap roots, nor the tops close enough to cause any "bleeding."

Brussels sprouts:—These are improved by freezing, and may be used from the open garden until December. If wanted later, store them with cabbage, or hang up the stalks in bunches in a cold cellar.

Cabbage:—If only a few heads are to be stored, a cool cellar will do. Even if where they will be slightly frozen, they will not be injured, so long as they do not freeze and thaw repeatedly. They should not be taken in until there is danger of severe freezing, as they will keep better, and a little frost improves the flavor. For storing small quantities outdoors, dig a trench, a foot or so deep, in a well-drained spot, wide enough to admit two heads side by side. Pull up the cabbages, without removing either stems or outer leaves, and store side by side, head down, in the bottom of the trench. Now cover over lightly with straw, meadow hay, or any refuse which will keep the dirt from freezing to the cabbages, and then cover over the whole with earth, to the depth of several inches, but allowing the top of the roots to remain exposed, which will facilitate digging them up as required. Do not bury the cabbage until as late as possible before severe freezing, as a spell of warm weather would rot it.

Carrots:—Treat in the same way as beets. They will not be hurt by a slight freezing of the tops, before being dug, but care must be taken not to let the roots become touched by frost.

Celery:—That which is to be used early is blanched outside, by banking, as described in Chapter XI, and as celery will stand a little freezing, will be used directly from the garden. For the portion to be kept over winter, provide boxes about a foot wide, and nearly as deep as the celery is high. Cover the bottoms of these boxes with two or three inches of sand, and wet thoroughly. Upon this stand the celery upright, and packed close together. In taking up the celery for storing in this way, the roots and whatever earth adheres to them are kept on, not cut, as it is bought in the stores. The boxes are then stored in a cellar, or other dark, dry, cold place where the temperature will not go more than five degrees below freezing. The celery will be ready for use after Christmas. If a long succession is wanted, store from the open two or three different times, say at the end of October, first part of November and the latter part of November.

Cucumbers, Melons, Egg-plant:—While there is no way of storing these for any great length of time without recourse to artificial cold, they may be had for some time by storing just before the first frosts in a cool, dark cellar, care being taken in handling the fruits to give them no bruises.

Onions:—If the onions got a good early start in the spring, the tops will begin to die down by the middle of August. As soon as the tops have turned yellow and withered they should be pulled, on the first clear dry day, and laid in windrows (three or four rows in one), but not heaped up. They should be turned over frequently, by hand or with a wooden rake, and removed to a shed or barn floor as soon as dry, where the tops can be cut off. Keep them spread out as much as possible, and give them open ventilation until danger of frost. Then store in a dry place and keep as cool as possible without freezing. A few barrels, with holes knocked in the sides, will do well for a small quantity.

Parsley:—Take up a few plants and keep in a flower-pot or small box, in the kitchen window.

Parsnips:—These will stay in the ground without injury all winter, but part of the crop may be taken up late in the fall and stored with beets, carrots and turnips, to use while the ground is frozen.

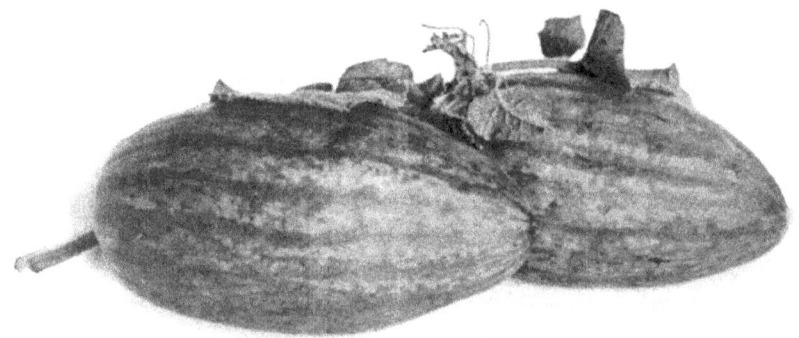

Delicata squash: one of the very best for the small garden, good for both summer and winter

Potatoes:—When the vines have died down and the skin of the new potatoes has become somewhat hardened, they can be dug and stored in a cool, dry cellar at once. Be sure to give plenty of ventilation until danger of frost. Keep from the light, as this has the effect of making the potatoes bitter. If there is any sign of rot among the tubers, do not dig them up until it has stopped.

Squash and Pumpkins:—The proper conditions for storing for winter will be indicated by the drying and shrinking of the stem. Cut them from the vines, being careful never to break off the stem, turn over, rub off the dirt and leave the underside exposed to a few days' sunlight. Then carry in a spring wagon, or spring wheelbarrow, covered with old bags or hay to keep from any bruises. Store in the dryest part of the cellar, and if possible where the temperature will not go below forty degrees. Leave them on the vines in the field as late as possible, while escaping frosts.

Tomatoes:—Just before the first frosts are likely to begin, pick all of the best of the unripened fruits. Place part of these on clean straw in a coldframe, giving protection, where they will gradually ripen up. Place others, that are fully developed but not ripe, in straw in the cellar. In this way fresh tomatoes may frequently be had as late as Christmas.

Turnip:—These roots, if desired, can be stored as are beets or carrots.

It is hard to retain our interest in a thing when most of its usefulness has gone by. It is for that reason, I suppose, that one sees so many forsaken and weed-grown gardens every autumn, where in the spring everything was neat and clean. But there are two very excellent reasons why the vegetable garden should not be so abandoned—to say nothing of appearances! The first is that many vegetables continue to grow until the heavy frosts come; and the second, that the careless gardener who thus forsakes his post is sowing no end of trouble for himself for the coming year. For weeds left to themselves, even late in the fall, grow in the cool moist weather with astonishing rapidity, and, almost before one realizes it, transform the well kept garden into a ragged wilderness, where the intruders have taken such a strong foothold that they cannot be pulled up without tearing everything else with them. So we let them go—and, left to themselves, they accomplish their purpose in life, and leave upon the ground an evenly distributed supply of plump ripe seeds, which next spring will cause the perennial exclamation, "Mercy, John, where did all these weeds come from?" And John replies, "I don't know; we kept the garden clean last summer. I think there must be weed seeds in the fertilizer."

Do not let up on your fight with weeds, for every good vegetable that is left over can be put to some use. Here and there in the garden will be a strip that has gone by, and as it is now too late to plant, we just let it go. Yet now is the time we should be preparing all such spots for withstanding next summer's drouth! You may remember how strongly was emphasized the necessity for having abundant humus (decayed vegetable matter) in the soil—how it acts like a sponge to retain moisture and keep things growing through the long, dry spells which we seem to be sure of getting every summer. So take thought for next year. Buy a bushel of rye, and as fast as a spot in your garden can be cleaned up, harrow, dig or rake it over, and sow the rye on broadcast. Just enough loose surface dirt to cover it and let it sprout, is all it asks. If the weather is dry, and you can get a small roller, roll it in to ensure better germination. It will come up quickly; it will keep out the weeds which otherwise would be taking possession of the ground; it will grow until the ground is frozen solid and begin again with the first warm spring day; it will keep your garden from washing out in heavy rains, and capture and save from being washed away and wasted a good deal of left-over plant food; it will serve as just so much real manure for your garden; it will improve the mechanical condition of the soil, and it will add the important element of humus to it.

In addition to these things, you will have an attractive and luxuriant garden spot, instead of an unsightly bare one. And in clearing off these patches for rye, beware of waste. If you have hens, or by chance a pig, they will relish old heads of lettuce, old pea-vines, still green after the last picking, and the stumps and outer leaves of cabbage. Even if you have not this means of utilizing your garden's by- products, do not let them go to waste. Put everything into a square pile—old sods, weeds, vegetable tops, refuse, dirt, leaves, lawn sweepings—anything that will rot. Tread this pile down thoroughly; give it a soaking once in a while if within reach of the hose, and two or three turnings with a fork. Next spring when you are looking for every available pound of manure with which to enrich your garden, this compost heap will stand you in good stead.

A very decisive answer to the "no room for fruit" argument

One way of finding room—standard grafted on dwarf stock

HOME VEGETABLE GARDENING

Trained fruit trees serving a double purpose; ornament in the spring and fruit in the fall

Burn now your old pea-brush, tomato poles and everything that is not worth keeping over for next year. Do not leave these things lying around to harbor and protect eggs and insects and weed seeds. If any bean-poles, stakes, trellises or supports seem in good enough condition to serve another year, put them under cover now; and see that all your tools are picked up and put in one place, where you can find them and overhaul them next February. As soon as your surplus pole beans have dried in their pods, take up poles and all and store in a dry place. The beans may be taken off later at your leisure.

Be careful to cut down and burn (or put in the compost heap) all weeds around your fences, and the edges of your garden, before they ripen seed.

If the suggestions given are followed, the vegetable garden may be stretched far into the winter. But do not rest at that. Begin to plan now for your next year's garden. Put a pile of dirt where it will not be frozen, or dried out, when you want to use it next February for your early seeds. If you have no hotbed, fix the frames and get the sashes for one now, so it will be ready to hand when the ground is frozen solid and covered with snow next spring. If you have made garden mistakes this year, be planning now to rectify them next—without progress there is no fun in the game. Let next spring find you with your plans all made, your materials all on hand and a fixed resolution to have the best garden you have ever had.

Part 3

Fruits and Berries

Chapter 15

The Varieties of Pome and Stone Fruits

Many a home gardener who has succeeded well with vegetables is, for some reason or other, still fearsome about trying his hand at growing his own fruit.

This is all a mistake; the initial expense is very slight (fruit trees will cost but twenty-five to forty cents each, and the berry bushes only about four cents each), and the same amount of care that is demanded by vegetables, if given to fruit, will produce apples, peaches, pears and berries far superior to any that can be bought, especially in flavor.

I know a doctor in New York, a specialist, who has attained prominence in his profession, and who makes a large income; he tells me that there is nothing in the city that hurts him so much as to have to pay out a nickel whenever he wants an apple. His boyhood home was on a Pennsylvania farm, where apples were as free as water, and he cannot get over the idea of their being one of Nature's gracious gifts, any more than he can overcome his hankering for that crisp, juicy, uncloying flavor of a good apple, which is not quite equaled by the taste of any other fruit.

And yet it is not the saving in expense, although that is considerable, that makes the strongest argument for growing one's own fruit. There are three other reasons, each of more importance. First is quality. The commercial grower cannot afford to grow the very finest fruit. Many of the best varieties are not large enough yielders to be available for his use, and he cannot, on a large scale, so prune and care for his trees that the individual fruits receive the greatest possible amount of sunshine and thinning out—the personal care that is required for the very best quality. Second, there is the beauty and the value that well-kept fruit trees add to a place, no matter how small it is. An apple tree in full bloom is one of the most beautiful pictures that Nature ever paints; and if, through any train of circumstances, it ever becomes advisable to sell or rent the home, its desirability is greatly enhanced by the few trees necessary to furnish the loveliness of showering blossoms in spring, welcome shade in summer and an abundance of delicious fruits through autumn and winter. Then there is the fun of doing it—of planting and caring for a few young trees, which will reward your labors, in a cumulative way, for many years to come.

But enough of reasons. If the call of the soil is in your veins, if your fingers (and your brain) in the springtime itch to have a part in earth's ever-wonderful renascence, if your lips part at the thought of the white, firm, toothsome flesh of a ripened-on-the-tree red apple— then you must have a home orchard without delay.

And it is not a difficult task. Apples, pears and the stone fruits, fortunately, are not very particular about their soils. They take kindly to anything between a sandy soil so loose as to be almost shifting, and heavy clay. Even these soils can be made available, but of course not without more work. And you need little room to grow all the fruit your family can possibly eat.

Time was, when to speak of an apple tree brought to mind one of those old, moss-barked giants that served as a carriage shed and a summer dining-room, decorated with scythes and rope swings, requiring the services of a forty-foot ladder and a long-handled picker to gather the fruit. That day is gone. In its stead have come the low-headed standard and the dwarf forms. The new types came as new institutions usually do, under protest. The wise said they would never be practical—the trees would not get large enough and teams could not be driven under them. But the facts remained that the low trees are more easily and thoroughly cared for; that they do not take up so much room; that they are less exposed to high winds, and such fruit as does fall is not injured; that the low limbs shelter the roots and conserve moisture; and, above all, that picking can be accomplished much more easily and with less injury to fine, well ripened fruit. The low-headed tree has come to stay.

If your space will allow, the low-headed standards will give you better satisfaction than the dwarfs. They are longer-lived, they are healthier, and they do not require nearly so much intensive culture. On the other hand, the dwarfs may be used where there is little or no room for the standards. If there is no other space available, they may be put in the vegetable or flower garden, and incidentally they are then sure of receiving some of that special care which they need in the way of fertilization and cultivation.

As I have said, any average soil will grow good fruit. A gravelly loam, with a gravel subsoil, is the ideal. Do not think from this, however, that all you have to do is buy a few trees from a nursery agent, stick them in the ground and from your negligence reap the rewards that follow only intelligent industry. The soil is but the raw material which work and care alone can transform, through the medium of the growing tree, into the desired result of a cellar well stored each autumn with fruit.

Fruit trees have one big advantage over vegetables—the ground can be prepared for them while they are growing. If the soil will grow a crop of clover it is already in good shape to furnish the trees with food at once. If not, manure or fertilizers may be applied, and clover or other green crops turned under during the first two or three years of the trees' growth, as will be described later.

The first thing to consider, when you have decided to plant, is the location you will give your trees. Plan to have pears, plums, cherries and peaches, as well as apples. For any of these the soil, of whatever nature, must be well drained. If not naturally, then tile or other artificial drainage must be provided. For only a few trees it would probably answer the purpose to dig out large holes and fill in a foot or eighteen inches at the bottom with small stone, covered with gravel or screened coal-cinders.

HOME VEGETABLE GARDENING

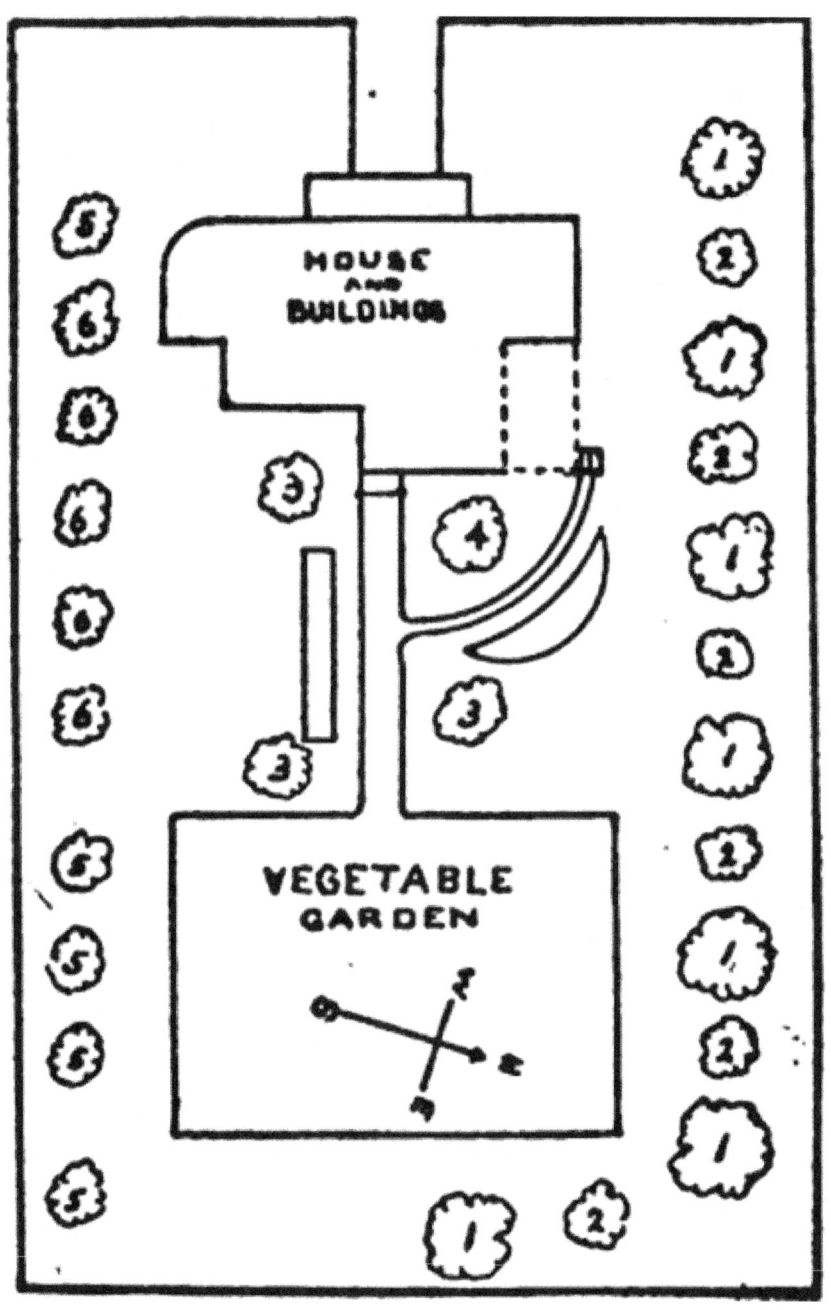

My own land has a gravelly subsoil and I have not had to drain. Then with the apples, and especially with the peaches, a too-sheltered slope to the south is likely to start the flower buds prematurely in spring, only to result in total crop loss from late frosts. The diagram on the next page suggests an arrangement which may be adapted to individual needs. One may see from it that the apples are placed to the north, where they will to some extent shelter the rest of the grounds; the peaches where they will not be coddled; the pears, which may be had upon quince stock, where they will not shade the vegetable garden; the cherries, which are the most ornamental, where they may lend a decorative effect.

And now, having decided that we can—and will—grow good fruit, and having in mind suggestions that will enable us to go out to-morrow morning and, with an armful of stakes, mark out the locations, the next consideration should be the all-important question of what varieties are most successfully grown on the small place.

The following selections are made with the home fruit garden, not the commercial orchard, in mind. While they are all "tried and true" sorts, succeeding generally in the northeast, New England and western fruit sections, remember that fruits, as a rule, though not so particular as vegetables about soil, seem much more so about locality. I would suggest, therefore, submitting your list, before buying, to your State Experiment Station. You are taxed for its support; get some direct result from it. There they will be glad to advise you, and are in the best position to help you get started properly. Above all, do not buy from the traveling nursery agent, with his grip full of wonderful lithographs of new and unheard-of novelties. Get the catalogue of several reliable nurseries, take standard varieties about which you know, and buy direct. Several years ago I had the opportunity to go carefully over one of the largest fruit nurseries in the country. Every care and precaution was taken to grow fine, healthy, young trees. The president told me that they sold thousands every year to smaller concerns, to be resold again through field and local agents. Yet they do an enormous retail business themselves, and of course their own customers get the best trees.

The following are listed, as nearly as I can judge, in the order of their popularity, but as many of the best are not valuable commercially, they are little known. Whenever you find a particularly good apple or pear, try to trace it, and add it to your list.

APPLES

Without any question, the apple is far and away the most valuable fruit, both because of its greater scope of usefulness and its longer season—the last of the winter's Russets are still juicy and firm when the first Early Harvests and Red Astrachans are tempting the "young idea" to experiment with colic. Plant but a small proportion of early varieties, for the late ones are better. Out of a dozen trees, I would put in one early, three fall, and the rest winter sorts.

Among the summer apples are several deserving special mention: Yellow Transparent is the earliest. It is an old favorite and one of the most easily grown of all apples. Its color is indicated by the name, and it is a fair eating-apple and a very good cooker. Red Astrachan, another first early, is not quite so good for cooking, but is a delicious eating-apple of good size. An apple of more recent introduction and extremely hardy (hailing first from Russia), and already replacing the above sorts, is Livland (Livland Raspberry). The tree is of good form, very vigorous and healthy. The fruit is ready almost as soon as Yellow Transparent, and is of much better quality for eating. In appearance it is exceptionally handsome, being of good size, regular form and having those beautiful red shades found almost exclusively in the later apples. The flesh is quality is fully up to its appearance. The white, crisp-breaking flesh, most aromatic, deliciously sub-acid, makes it ideal for eating. A neighbor of mine sold $406 worth of fruit from twenty trees to one dealer. For such a splendid apple McIntosh is remarkably hardy and vigorous, succeeding over a very wide territory, and climate severe enough to kill many of the other newer varieties. The Fameuse (widely known as the Snow) is an excellent variety for northern sections. It resembles the McIntosh, which some claim to be derived from it. Fall Pippin, Pound Sweet and Twenty Ounce, are other popular late autumns.

In the winter section, Baldwin, which is too well known to need describing, is the leading commercial variety in many apple districts, and it is a good variety for home growing on account of its hardiness and good cooking and keeping qualities; but for the home orchard, it is far surpassed in quality by several others. In northern sections, down to the corn line, Northern Spy is a great favorite. It is a large, roundish apple, with thin, tender, glossy skin, light to deep carmine over light yellow, and an excellent keeper. In sections to which it is adapted it is a particularly vigorous, compact, upright grower. Jonathan is another splendid sort, with a wider range of conditions favorable for growth. It is, however, not a strong-growing tree and is somewhat uncertain in maturing its fruit, which is a bright, clear red of distinctive flavor. It likes a soil with more clay than do most apples. In the Middle West and Middle South, Grimes (Golden) has made a great local reputation in many sections, although in others it has not done well at all.

The Spitzenberg (Esopus) is very near the top of the list of all late eating-apples, being at its prime about December. It is another handsome yellow-covered red apple, with flesh slightly yellowish, but very good to the taste. The tree, unfortunately, is not a robust grower, being especially weak in its earlier stages, but with good cultivation it will not fail to reward the grower for any extra care it may have required.

These, and the other notable varieties, which there is not room here to describe, make up the following list, from which the planter should select according to locality:

Earliest or Summer:—Early Harvest, Yellow Transparent, Red Astrachan, Benoni (new), Chenango, Sweet Bough, Williams' Favorite, Early Strawberry, Livland Raspberry.

Early Autumn:—Alexander, Duchess, Porter, Gravenstein, McIntosh Red.

Late Autumn:—Jefferies, Fameuse (Snow), Maiden's Blush, Wealthy, Fall Pippin, Pound Sweet, Twenty Ounce, Cox Orange, Hubbardston.

Winter:—Baldwin, Rhode Island Greening, Northwestern Greening, Jonathan, Northern Spy, Yellow, Swaar, Delicious, Wagener, King, Esopus, Spitzenberg, Yellow Bellflower, Winter Banana, Seek-no-further, Talman Sweet, Roxbury Russett, King David, Stayman's Winesap, Wolf River.

PEARS

Pears are more particular than apples in the matter of being adapted to sections and soils. Submit your list to your State Experiment Station before ordering trees. Many of the standard sorts may be had where a low-growing, spreading tree is desired (for instance, quince-stock pears might be used to change places with the plums). Varieties suitable for this method are listed below. They are given approximately in the order of the ripening:

Wilder: Early August, medium in size, light yellow, excellent quality. Does not rot at the core, as so many early pears are liable to do.

Margaret: Oblong, greenish, yellow to dull red.

Clapp Favorite: Very large, yellow pear. A great bearer and good keeper —where the children cannot get at it.

Howell: A little later than the foregoing; large, bright yellow, strong-growing tree and big bearer.

Duchesse d'Angouleme: Large greenish yellow, sometimes reaching huge size; will average better than three-quarters of a pound. The quality, despite its size, is splendid.

Seckel: Small in size, but renowned for exquisite flavor—being probably the most universally admired of all.

Beurre Superfine: October, medium size, excellent quality.

Bartlett: The best known of all pears, and a universal favorite. Succeeds in nearly all sections.

Anjou: One of the best keepers, and very productive. One of the best in flavor, rich and vinous.

For trees of the standard type the following are worthy of note:

Congress (Souvenir du C.): A very large summer sort. Handsome.

Belle Lucrative: September to October.

Winter Nelis: Medium size, but of excellent quality and the longest keeper.

Kieffer: Very popular for its productiveness, strength of growth and exceptional quality of fruit for canning and preserving. Large fruit, if kept thinned. Should have a place in every home garden.

Josephine de Malines: Not a great yielder but of the very highest quality, being of the finest texture and tempting aroma.

Peach trees come into bearing in three years, so they are frequently used as "fillers" between the rows of slower trees

Two crops on the same ground at the same time—fruit and poultry. The chickens help to keep in check the devastating hordes of insects

A plum tree in full bearing. Low-headed trees are come to stay. They are less liable to damage by wind and facilitate the gathering of fruit

PEACHES

Success with peaches also will depend largely upon getting varieties adapted to climate. The white-fleshed type is the hardiest and best for eating; and the free-stones are for most purposes, especially in the home garden, more desirable than the "clings."

Greensboro is the best early variety. Crawford is a universal favorite and goes well over a wide range of soil and climate. Champion is one of the best quality peaches and exceptionally hardy. Elberta, Ray, and Hague are other excellent sorts. Mayflower is the earliest sort yet introduced.

PLUMS

The available plums are of three classes—the natives, Europeans and Japans; the natives are the longest-lived, hardier in tree and blossom, and heavier bearers.

The best early is Milton; brilliant red, yellow and juicy flesh. Wild-goose and Whitaker are good seconds. Mrs. Cleveland is a later and larger sort, of finer quality. Three late-ripening plums of the finest quality, but not such prolific yielders, are Wayland, Benson and Reed, and where there is room for only a few trees, these will be best. They will need one tree of Newman or Prairie Flower with them to assure setting of the fruit. Of the Europeans, use Reine Claude (the best), Bradshaw or Shropshire. Damson is also good. The Japanese varieties should go on high ground and be thinned, especially during their first years. My first experience with Japanese plums convinced me that I had solved the plum problem; they bore loads of fruit, and were free from disease. That was five years ago. Last spring the last one was cut and burned. Had they been planted at the top of a small hill, instead of at the bottom, as they were, and restricted in their bearing, I know from later experience that they would still be producing fruit. The most satisfactory varieties of the Japanese type are Abundance and Red June. Burbank is also highly recommended,

F. F. ROCKWELL

CHERRIES

Cherries have one advantage over the other fruits—they give quicker returns. But, as far as my experience goes, they are not as long-lived. The sour type is hardier, at least north of New Jersey, than the sweet. It will probably pay to try a few of the new and highly recommended varieties. Of the established sorts Early Richmond is a good early, to be followed by Montmorency and English Morello. Windsor is a good sweet cherry, as are also Black Tartarian, Sox, Wood and Yellow Spanish.

All the varieties mentioned above are proved sorts. But the lists are being added to constantly, and where there is a novelty strongly recommended by a reliable nurseryman it will often pay to try it out—on a very small scale at first.

Chapter 16

Planting: Cultivation for Filler Tops

As the pedigree and the quality of the stock you plant will have a great deal to do with the success or failure of your adventure in orcharding, even on a very small scale, it is important to get the best trees you can, anywhere, at any price. But do not jump to the conclusion that the most costly trees will be the best. From reliable nurserymen, selling direct by mail, you can get good trees at very reasonable prices.

As a general thing you will succeed best if you have nothing to do with the perennial "tree agent." He may represent a good firm; you may get your trees on time; he may have a novelty as good as the standard sorts; but you are taking three very great chances in assuming so. But, leaving these questions aside, there is no particular reason why you should help pay his traveling expenses and the printing bills for his lithographs ("made from actual photographs" or "painted from nature," of course!) when you can get the best trees to be had, direct from the soil in which they are grown, at the lowest prices, by ordering through the mail. Or, better still, if the nursery is not too far away, take half a day off and select them in person. If you want to help the agent along present him with the amount of his commission, but get your trees direct from some large reliable nursery.

Well grown nursery stock will stand much abuse, but it will not be at all improved by it. Do not let yours stand around in the sun and wind, waiting until you get a chance to set it out. As soon as you get it home from the express office, unpack it and "heel it in," in moist, but not wet, ground; if under a shed, so much the better. Dig out a narrow trench and pack it in as thick as it will go, at an angle of forty-five degrees to the natural position when growing. So stored, it will keep a long time in cold weather, only be careful that no rats, mice, or rabbits reach it.

Do not, however, depend upon this knowledge to the extent of letting all your preparations for planting go until your stock is on hand. Be ready to set it the day it arrives, if possible.

PLANTING

Planting can be done in either spring or fall. As a general rule, north of Philadelphia and St. Louis, spring planting will be best; south of that, fall planting. Where there is apt to be severe freezing, "heaving," caused by the alternate freezing and thawing; injury to the newly set roots from too severe cold; and, in some western sections, "sun-scald" of the bark, are three injuries which may result. If trees are planted in the fall in cold sections, a low mound of earth, six to twelve inches high, should be left during the winter about each, and leveled down in the spring. If set in the spring, where hot, dry weather is apt to follow, they should be thoroughly mulched with litter, straw or coarse manure, to preserve moisture—care being taken, however, against field mice and other rodents.

The trees may either be set in their permanent positions as soon as bought, or grown in "nursery rows" by the purchaser for one or two years after being purchased. In the former case, it will be the best policy to get the strongest, straightest two-year stock you can find, even if they cost ten or fifteen cents apiece more than the "mediums." The former method is the usual one, but the latter has so many advantages that I give it the emphasis of a separate paragraph, and urge every prospective planter to consider it carefully.

In the first place, then, you get your trees a little cheaper. If you purchase for nursery row planting, six-foot to seven-foot two-year-old apple trees, of the standard sorts, should cost you about thirty cents each; one-year "buds," six feet and branched, five to ten cents less. This gain, however, is not an important one—there are four others, each of which makes it worthwhile to give the method a trial. First, the trees being all together, and in a convenient place, the chances are a hundred to one that you will give them better attention in the way of spraying, pruning and cultivating—all extremely important in the first year's growth. Second, with the year gained for extra preparation of the soil where they are to be placed permanently, you can make conditions just right for them to take hold at once and thrive as they could not do otherwise. Third, the shock of transplanting will be much less than when they are shipped from a distance—they will have made an additional growth of dense, short roots and they will have become acclimated. Fourth, you will not have wasted space and time with any backward black sheep among the lot, as these should be discarded at the second planting. And then there is one further reason, psychological perhaps, but none the less important; you will watch these little trees, which are largely the result of your own labor and care, when set in their permanent positions, much more carefully than you would those direct from the nursery. I know, both from experience and observation, how many thrifty young trees in the home orchard are done to an untimely death by children, careless workmen, and other animals.

So if you can put a twelve-month curb on your impatience, get one-year trees and set them out in a straight row right in your vegetable garden where they will take up very little room. Keep them cultivated just as thoroughly as the rest of your growing things. Melons, or beans, or almost any low-growing vegetable can be grown close beside them.

If you want your garden to pay for your whole lot of fruit trees this season dig up a hole about three feet in diameter wherever a tree is to "go permanently." Cut the sod up fine and work in four or five good forkfuls of well rotted manure, and on these places, when it is warm enough, plant a hill of lima pole-beans-the new sort named Giant-podded Pole Lima is the best I have yet seen. Place a stout pole, eight to ten feet high, firmly in each hole. Good lima beans are always in demand, and bring high prices.

Let us suppose that your trees are at hand, either direct from the nursery or growing in the garden. You have selected, if possible, a moist, gravelly loam on a slope or slight elevation, where it is naturally and perfectly drained. Good soil drainage is imperative. Coarse gravel in the bottom of the planting hole will help out temporarily. If the land is in clover sod, it will have the ideal preparation, especially if you can grow a patch of potatoes or corn on it one year, while your trees are getting further growth. In such land the holes will not have to be prepared. If, however, you are not fortunate enough to be able to devote such a space to fruit trees, and in order to have them at all must place them along your wall or scattered through the grounds, you can still give them an excellent start by enriching the soil in spots beforehand, as suggested above in growing lima beans. In the event of finding even this last way inapplicable to your land, the following method will make success certain: Dig out holes three to six feet in diameter (if the soil is very hard, the larger dimension), and twelve to eighteen inches deep. Mix thoroughly with the excavated soil a good barrowful of the oldest, finest manure you can get, combined with about one-fourth or one-fifth its weight of South Carolina rock (or acid phosphate, if you cannot get the rock). It is a good plan to compost the manure and rock in advance, or use the rock as an absorbent in the stable. Fill in the hole again, leaving room in the center to set the tree without bending or cramping any roots. Where any of these are injured or bruised, cut them off clean at the injured spot with a sharp knife. Shorten any that are long and straggling about one-third to one-half their length. Properly grown stock should not be in any such condition.

Remember that a well planted tree will give more fruit in the first ten years than three trees carelessly put in. Get the tree so that it will be one to three inches deeper in the soil than when growing in the nursery. Work the soil in firmly about the roots with the fingers or a blunt wooden "tamper"; do not be afraid to use your feet. When the roots are well covered, firm the tree in by putting all your weight upon the soil around it. See that it is planted straight, and if the "whip," or small trunk, is not straight stake it, and tie it with rye straw, raffia or strips of old cloth-never string or wire. If the soil is very dry, water the root copiously while planting until the soil is about half filled in, never on the surface, as that is likely to cause a crust to form and keep out the air so necessary to healthy growth.

Prune back the "leader" of the tree-the top above the first lateral branches, about one-half. Peach trees should be cut back more severely. Further information in regard to pruning, and the different needs of the various fruits in regard to this important matter, will be given in the next chapter.

SETTING

Standard apple trees, fully grown, will require thirty to forty-five feet of space between them each way. It takes, however, ten or twelve years after the trees are set before all of this space is needed. A system of "fillers," or inter-planting, has come into use as a result of this, which will give at least one hundred per cent, more fruit for the first ten years. Small-growing standards, standard varieties on dwarf stock, and also peaches, are used for this purpose in commercial orchards. But the principle may be applied with equally good results to the home orchard, or even to the planting of a few scattered trees. The standard dwarfs give good satisfaction as permanent fillers. Where space is very limited, or the fruit must go into the garden, they may be used in place of the standard sorts altogether. The dwarf trees are, as a rule, not so long-lived as the standards, and to do their best, need more care in fertilizing and manuring; but the fruit is just as good; just as much, or more, can be grown on the same area; and the trees come into bearing two to three years sooner. They cost less to begin with and are also easier to care for, in spraying and pruning and in picking the fruit.

CULTIVATION

The home orchard, to give the very finest quality of fruit, must be given careful and thorough cultivation. In the case of scattered trees, where it is not practicable to use a horse, this can be given by working a space four to six feet wide about each tree. Every spring the soil should be loosened up, with the cultivator or fork, as the case may be, and kept stirred during the early part of the summer. Unless the soil is rich, a fertilizer, high in potash and not too high in nitrogen, should be given in the spring. Manure and phosphate rock, as suggested above, is as good as any. In case the foliage is not a deep healthy green, apply a few handfuls of nitrate of soda, working it into the soil just before a rain, around each tree.

About August 1st the cultivation should be discontinued, and some "cover crop" sown. Buckwheat and crimson clover is a good combination; as the former makes a rapid growth it will form, if rolled down just as the apples are ripening, a soft cushion upon which the windfalls may drop without injury, and will furnish enough protection to the crimson clover to carry it through most winters, even in cold climates.

In addition to the filler crops, where the ground is to be cultivated by horse, potatoes may be grown between the rows of trees; or fine hills of melons or squash may be grown around scattered trees, thus, incidentally, saving a great deal of space in the vegetable garden. Or why not grow a few extra fancy strawberries in the well cultivated spots about these trees? Neither they nor the trees want the ground too rich, especially in nitrogen, and conditions suiting the one would be just right for the others.

It may seem to the beginner that fruit-growing, with all these things to keep in mind, is a difficult task. But it is not. I think I am perfectly safe in saying that the rewards from nothing else he can plant and care for are as certain, and surely none are more satisfactory. If you cannot persuade yourself to try fruit on any larger plan, at least order half a dozen dwarf trees (they will cost about twenty cents apiece, and can be had by mail). They will prove about the best paying investment you ever made.

Chapter 17

Pruning, Spraying, and Harvesting

The day has gone, probably forever, when setting out fruit trees and giving them occasional cultivation, "plowing up the orchard" once in several years, would produce fruit. Apples and pears and peaches have occupied no preferred position against the general invasion of the realm of horticulture by insect and fungous enemies. The fruits have, indeed, suffered more than most plants. Nevertheless there is this encouraging fact: that, though the fruits may have been severely attacked, the means we now have of fighting fruit-tree enemies, if thoroughly used, as a rule are more certain of accomplishing their purpose, and keeping the enemies completely at bay, than are similar weapons in any other line of horticultural work.

With fruit trees, as with vegetables and flowers, the most important precaution to be taken against insects and disease is to have them in a healthy, thriving, growing condition. It is a part of Nature's law of the survival of the fittest that any backward or weakling plant or tree seems to fall first prey to the ravages of destructive forces.

For these reasons the double necessity of maintaining at all times good fertilization and thorough cultivation will be seen. In addition to these two factors, careful attention in the matter of pruning is essential in keeping the trees in a healthy, robust condition. As explained in a previous chapter, the trees should be started right by pruning the first season to the open-head or vase shape, which furnishes the maximum of light and air to all parts of the tree. Three or four main branches should form the basis of the head, care being taken not to have them start from directly opposite points on the trunk, thus forming a crotch and leaving the tree liable to splitting from winds or excessive crops. If the tree is once started right, further pruning will give little trouble. Cut out limbs which cross, or are likely to rub against each other, or that are too close together; and also any that are broken, decayed, or injured in any way. For trees thus given proper attention from the start, a short jackknife will be the only pruning instrument required.

The case of the old orchard is more difficult. Cutting out too many of the old, large limbs at one time is sure to give a severe shock to the vitality of the tree. A better plan is, first, to cut off close all suckers and all small new-growth limbs, except a few of the most promising, which may be left to be developed into large limbs; and then as these new limbs grow on, gradually to cut out, using a fine-tooth saw and painting the exposed surfaces, the surplus old wood. Apples will need more pruning than the other fruits. Pears and cherries need the least; cutting back the ends of limbs enough to keep the trees in good form, with the removal of an occasional branch for the purpose of letting in light and air, is all the pruning they will require. Of course trees growing on rich ground, and well cultivated, will require more cutting back than those growing under poorer conditions. A further purpose of pruning is to effect indirectly a thinning of the fruit, so that what is grown will be larger and more valuable, and also that the trees may not become exhausted by a few exceptionally heavy crops. On trees that have been neglected and growing slowly the bark sometimes becomes hard and set. In such cases it will prove beneficial to scrape the bark and give a wash applied with an old broom. Whitewash is good for this purpose, but soda or lye answers the same purpose and is less disagreeably conspicuous. Slitting the bark of trunks and the largest limbs is sometimes resorted to, care being taken to cut through the bark only; but such practice is objectionable because it leaves ready access to some forms of fungous disease and to borers.

Where extra fine specimens of fruit are desired, thinning is practiced. It helps also to prevent the tree from being overtaxed by excessive crops. But where pruning is thoroughly done this trouble is usually avoided. Peaches and Japan plums are especially benefited by thinning, as they have a great tendency to overbear. The spread of fruit diseases, especially rot in the fruit itself, is also to some extent checked.

Of fruit-tree enemies there are some large sorts which may do great damage in short order—rabbits and field mice. They may be kept away by mechanical protection, such as wire, or by heaping the earth up to a height of twelve inches about the tree trunk. Or they may be caught with poisoned baits, such as boiled grain in which a little Rough on Rats or similar poison has been mixed. The former method for the small home garden is little trouble, safer to Fido and Tabby, and the most reliable in effect.

Insects and scale diseases are not so easily managed; and that brings us to the question of spraying and of sprays.

For large orchards the spray must, of course, be applied with powerful and expensive machinery. For the small fruit garden a much simpler and very moderate priced apparatus may be acquired. The most practical of these is the brass-tank compressed-air sprayer, with extension rod and mist-spray nozzle. Or one of the knapsack sprayers may be used. Either of these will be of great assistance not only with the fruit trees, but everywhere in the garden. With care they will last a good many years. Whatever type you get, be sure to get a brass machine; as cheaper ones, made of other metal, quickly corrode from contact with the strong poisons used.

APPLE ENEMIES

The insects most commonly attacking the apple are the codlin-moth, tent-caterpillar, canker-worm and borer. The codlin-moth lays its eggs on the fruit about the time of the falling of the blossoms, and the larvae when hatched eat into the young fruit and cause the ordinary wormy apples and pears. Owing to these facts, it is too late to reach the trouble by spraying after the calyx closes on the growing fruit. Keep close watch and spray immediately upon the fall of the blossoms, and repeat the spraying a week or so (not more than two) later. For spray use Paris green at the rate of 1 lb., or arsenate of lead (paste or powder, less of the latter: see accompanying directions) at the rate of 4 lbs. to 100 gallons of water, being careful to have a thorough mixture. During July, tie strips of burlap or old bags around the trunks, and every week or so destroy all caterpillars caught in these traps. The tent-caterpillar may be destroyed while in the egg state, as these are plainly visible around the smaller twigs in circular, brownish masses. (See illustration.) Upon hatching, also, the nests are obtrusively visible and may be wiped out with a swab of old bag, or burned with a kerosene torch. Be sure to apply this treatment before the caterpillar begins to leave the nest. The treatment recommended for codlin-moths is also effective for the tent-caterpillar.

The canker-worm is another leaf-feeding enemy, and can be taken care of by the Paris green or arsenate spray.

The railroad-worm, a small white maggot which eats a small path in all directions through the ripening fruit, cannot be reached by spraying, as he starts life inside the fruit; but where good clean tillage is practiced and no fallen fruit is left to lie and decay under the trees, he is not apt to give much trouble.

The borer's presence is indicated by the dead, withered appearance of the bark, beneath which he is at work, and also by small amounts of sawdust where he entered. Dig him out with a sharp pocket-knife, or kill him inside with a piece of wire.

The most troublesome disease of the apple, especially in wet seasons, is the apple-scab, which disfigures the fruit, both in size and in appearance, as it causes blotches and distortions. Spray with Bordeaux mixture, 5-5-50, or 3-3-50 (see formulas below) three times: just before the blossoms open, just as they fall, and ten days to two weeks after they fall. The second spraying is considered the most important.

Prune trees to secure an open center. Cut out all limbs that cross one another

The San José scale is of course really an insect, though in appearance it seems a disease. It is much more injurious than the untrained fruit grower would suppose, because indirectly so. It is very tiny, being round in outline, with a raised center, and only the size of a small pinhead. Where it has once obtained a good hold it multiplies very rapidly, makes a scaly formation or crust on the branches, and causes small red-edged spots on the fruit (see illustration). For trees once infested, spray thoroughly both in fall, after the leaves drop, and again in spring, before growth begins. Use lime-sulphur wash, or miscible oil, one part to ten of water, thoroughly mixed.

CHERRY ENEMIES

Sour cherries are more easily grown than the sweet varieties, and are less subject to the attacks of fruit enemies. Sweet cherries are troubled by the curculio, or fruit-worm, which attacks also peaches and plums. Cherries and plums may be sprayed, when most of the blossoms are off, with a strong arsenate of lead solution, 5 to 8 lbs. to 100 gals. water. In addition to this treatment, where the worms have once got a start, the beetles may be destroyed by spreading a sheet around and beneath the tree, and every day or so shaking or jarring them off into it, as described below.

PEACH ENEMIES

Do not spray peaches. For the curculio, within a few days after the flowers are off, take a large sheet of some cheap material to use as a catcher. For large orchards there is a contrivance of this sort, mounted on a wheelbarrow frame, but for the home orchard a couple of sheets laid upon the ground, or one with a slit from one side to the center, will answer. If four short, sharp-pointed stakes are fastened to the corners, and three or four stout hooks and eyes are placed to reunite the slit after the sheet is placed about the tree, the work can be more thoroughly done, especially on uneven ground. After the sheet is placed, with a stout club or mallet, padded with a heavy sack or something similar to prevent injury to the bark, give a few sharp blows, well up from the ground. This work should be done on a cloudy day, or early in the morning—the colder the better—as the beetles are then inactive. If a considerable number of beetles are caught the operation should be repeated every two or three days. Continue until the beetles disappear.

Peaches are troubled also by borers, in this case indicated by masses of gum, usually about the crown. Dig out or kill with a wire, as in the case of the apple-borer. Look over the trees for borers every spring, or better, every spring and fall.

Another peach enemy is the "yellows," indicated by premature ripening of the fruit and the formation of stunted leaf tufts, of a light yellow color. This disease is contagious and has frequently worked havoc in whole sections. Owing to the work of the Agricultural Department and the various State organizations it is now held in check. The only remedy is to cut and burn the trees and replant, in the same places if desired, as, the disease does not seem to be carried by the soil.

PEAR ENEMIES

Pears are sometimes affected with a scab similar to the apple-scab, and this is combated by the same treatment—three sprayings with Bordeaux.

A blight which causes the leaves suddenly to turn black and die and also kills some small branches and produces sores or wounds on large branches and trunk, offers another difficulty. Cut out and burn all affected branches and scrape out all sores. Disinfect all sores with corrosive sublimate solution—1 to 1000—or with a torch, and paint over at once.

The efficiency of spraying depends upon the thoroughness with which the liquid is applied —cover every twig. A compressed air tank sprayer with extension rod is seen here

Prune trees to secure an open center. Cut out all limbs that cross one another

PLUM ENEMIES

Plums have many enemies but fortunately they can all be effectively checked. First is the curculio, to be treated as described above.

For leaf-blight—spotting and dropping off of the leaves about mid-summer—spray with Bordeaux within a week or so after the falling of the blossoms. This treatment will also help to prevent fruit-rot. In addition to the spraying, however, thin out the fruit so that it does not hang thickly enough for the plums to come in contact with each other.

In a well-kept and well sprayed orchard black-knot is not at all likely to appear. It is very manifest wherever it starts, causing ugly, black, distorted knarls, at first on the smaller limbs. Remove and burn immediately, and keep a sharp watch for more. As this disease is supposed to be carried by the wind, see to it that no careless neighbor is supplying you with the germs.

As will have been seen from the above, spraying poisons are of two kinds: those that work by contact, which must be used for most sucking insects, and germs and fungous diseases; and those that poison internally, used for leaf-eating insects. Of the former sort, Bordeaux mixture is the standard, although within the last few years it has been to a considerable extent replaced by lime-sulphur mixtures, which are described below. Bordeaux is made in various forms. That usually used is the 5-5-50, or 5 lbs. copper sulphate, 5 lbs. unslaked lime, 50 gals. water. To save the trouble of making up the mixture each time it is needed make a stock solution as follows: dissolve the copper sulphate in water at the rate of 1 lb. to 1 gal. This should be done the day before, or at least several hours before, the Bordeaux is wanted for use. Suspend the sulphate crystals in a cloth or old bag just below the surface of the water. Then slake the lime in a tub or tight box, adding the water a little at a time, until the whole attains the consistency of thick milk. When necessary, add water to this mixture if it is kept too long; never let it dry out. When ready to spray, pour the stock copper sulphate solution into the tank in the proportion of 5 gals. to every 50 of spray required. Add water to amount required. Then add stock lime solution, first diluting about one-half with water and straining. The amount of lime stock solution to be used is determined as follows: at the druggist's get an ounce of yellow prussiate of potash dissolved in a pint of water, with a quill in the cork of the bottle so that it may be dropped out. (It is poison.) When adding the stock lime solution as directed above, continue until the prussiate testing solution when dropped into the Bordeaux mixture will no longer turn brown; then add a little more lime to be on the safe side. All this sounds like a formidable task, but it is quite simple when you really get at it. Remember that all you need is a few pounds each of quicklime and copper sulphate, an ounce of prussiate of potash and a couple of old kegs or large pails, in which to keep the stock solutions,

Lime-sulphur mixtures can be bought, or mixed by the home orchardist. They have the advantages over Bordeaux that they do not discolor the foliage or affect the appearance of the fruit. Use according to directions, usually about 1 part to 30 of water. These may be used at the same times and for the same purposes as Bordeaux.

Lime-sulphur wash is used largely in commercial orcharding, but it is a nasty mess to prepare and must be used in late fall or winter. For the home orchard one of the miscible oils now advertised will be found more satisfactory. While they cost more, there is no time or expense for preparation, as they mix with cold water and are immediately ready for use. They are easier to apply, more comfortable to handle, and will not so quickly rot out pumps and spraying apparatus. Like the sulphur wash, use only during late fall and winter.

Kerosene emulsion is made by dissolving Ivory, soft, whale-oil, or tar soap in hot water and adding (away from the stove, please!) kerosene (or crude oil); 1/2 lb. soap, 1 gal. water, 2 gals, kerosene. Immediately place in a pail and churn or pump until a thick, lathery cream results. This is the stock solution: for use, dilute with five to fifteen times as much water, according to purpose applied for—on dormant fruit trees, 5 to 7 times; on foliage, 10 or even 15.

Of the poisons for eating-insects, arsenate of lead is the best for use in the fruit orchard, because it will not burn the foliage as Paris green is apt to do, and because it stays on longer. It can be used in Bordeaux and lime-sulphur mixtures, thus killing two bugs with one spray. It comes usually in the form of a paste—though there is now a brand in powder form (which I have not yet tried). This should be worked up with the fingers (it is not poison to touch) or a small wooden paddle, until thoroughly mixed, in a small quantity of water and then strained into the sprayer. Use, of the paste forms, from one-fourth to one lb. in 20 gals, clear water.

Paris green is the old standard. With a modern duster it may be blown on pure without burning, if carefully done. Applied thus it should be put on during a still morning, before the dew goes. It is safer to use as a spray, first making a paste with a small quantity of water, and then adding balance of water. Keep constantly stirred while spraying.

If lime is added, weight for weight with the green, the chances of burning will be greatly reduced. For orchard work, 1 lb. to 100 gals. water is the usual strength.

The accompanying table will enable the home orchardist to find quickly the trouble with, and remedy for, any of his fruit trees.

The quality of fruit will depend very largely upon the care exercised in picking and storing. Picking, carelessly done, while it may not at the time show any visible bad results, will result in poor keeping and rot. If the tissue cells are broken, as many will be by rough handling, they will be ready to cause rotten spots under the first favorable conditions, and then the rot will spread. Most of the fruits of the home garden, which do not have to undergo shipping, will be of better quality where they ripen fully on the tree. Pears, however, are often ripened in the dark and after picking, especially the winter sorts. Apples and pears for winter use should be kept, if possible, in a cold, dark place, where there is no artificial heat, and where the air will be moist, but never wet, and where the thermometer will not fall below thirty-two degrees. Upon exceptionally cold nights the temperature may be kept up by using an oil stove or letting in heat from the furnace cellar, if that is adjacent. In such a place, store the fruit loosely, on ventilated shelves, not more than six or eight inches deep. If they must be kept in a heated place, pack in tight boxes or barrels, being careful to put away only perfect fruit, or pack in sand or leaves. Otherwise they will lose much in quality by shriveling, due to lack of moisture in the atmosphere. With care they may be had in prime quality until late in the following spring.

Do not let yourself be discouraged from growing your own fruit by the necessity for taking good care of your trees. After all, you do not have to plant them every year, as you do vegetables, and they yield a splendid return on the small investment required. Do not fail to set out at least a few this year with the full assurance that your satisfaction is guaranteed by the facts in the case.

FRUIT	PEST	REMEDY	TIMES TO APPLY AND WHEN
Apple	Apple-scab	Bordeaux 5-5-50, or summer lime-sulphur spray	3.—b B O—a B F—f 14 d.
	Apple-maggot or Railroad worm	Pick up and destroy all fallen fruits	(See key below.)
	Borer	Dig out or kill with wire; search for in fall and spring	
	Codlin moth	Arsenate of lead, 4 in 100; or Paris Green, 1 in 100. Burlap bands on trunk for traps during July	2.—a B F—f 20 d.
	Cankerworm	Same as above	
	Tent-caterpillar	Same as above, also wipe out or burn nests	
	Blister-mite	Lime-sulphur wash; kerosene emulsion (dilute 5 times) or miscible oil (1 in 10 gal.)	Late fall or early spring.
	Bud-moth	Arsenate of lead or Paris Green	2—When leaves appear—b B O.
Cherry	Leaf blight	Bordeaux 5-5-50	4.—b B C—a calyx closes—f 15 d—f 15 d.
	Curculio	Arsenate of lead, 8 in 100. Curculio catcher (see Plum)	1.—a B F. 3 times a week.
	Black-knot	Cut out and burn at once (see Plum)	
	Fruit-rot	Pick before fully ripe. Spread out in cool, airy room	
Peach	Borer	Dig out or kill with wire	
	Yellows	Pull out and burn tree—replant	
	Curculio	Do not spray. Catch on sheets (see Plum)	
	Brown-rot	Summer lime-sulphur; open pruning; pick rotten fruit	3.—When fruit is half grown—f 10 d—f 10 d.
	Leaf-curl	Bordeaux 5-5-50; lime-sulphur wash	1—b buds swell, fall or early spring.
Pear	Blight	Cut out diseased branches; clean out sores; disinfect with corrosive sublimate 1 in 1000; paint over	
	Scab	Bordeaux 5-5-50, or summer sulphur (see Apple)	2.—b B O—a B O—f 14 d.
	Blister-mite		
Plum	Leaf-blight	Bordeaux or summer sulphur	1.—After fruits set.
	Fruit-rot	Same; also thin fruits so as not to touch (see Cherry) also have neighboring trees cleaned up	
	Black-knot		
	Curculio	Jar down on sheets stretched beneath trees and destroy	a B F—cool mornings—3 times a week.
Any	San José scale	Lime-sulphur wash, kerosene emulsion, 5 times diluted; miscible oil, 1 in 10 gals	Late fall or early spring.
	Oyster-shell scale	Kerosene emulsion	May or June, when young whitish lice appear.

a—After.   b—Before.   d—Days.   f—Follow up in.   B—Blossoms.   O—Open.   F—Fall.

Plums slightly infested with San José scal and its attendant discoloration

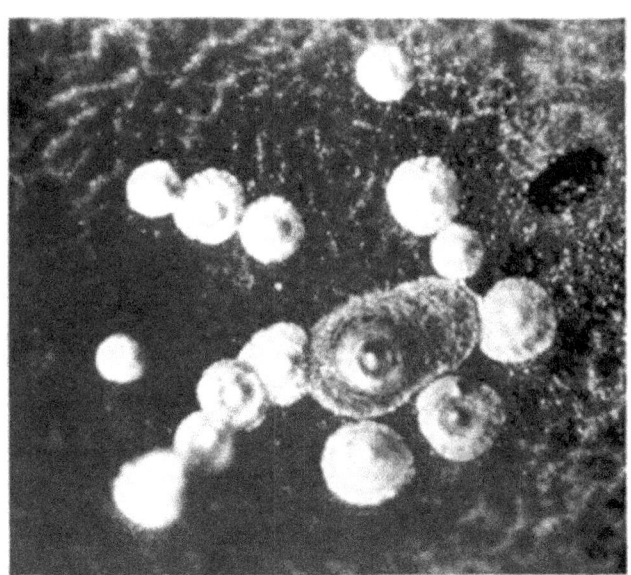

Male scale surrounded by young scales in various sizes—greatly enlarged

F. F. ROCKWELL

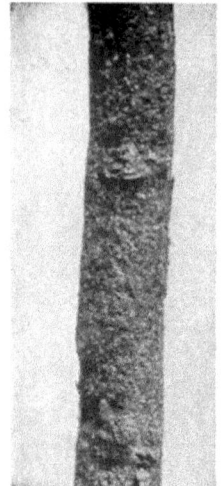  

Egg masses of the tent-caterpillar   Plum leaf attacked with San José scale.   Plum twig badly infested with San José scale

TWO OF THE COMMON FRUIT TREE ENEMIES

Chapter 18

Berries and Small Fruits

Besides the tree-fruits discussed in the preceding chapters, there is another class which should be represented in every home garden—the berries and small fruits. These have the advantage of occupying much less room than the former do and are therefore available where the others are not.

The methods of giving berries proper cultivation are not so generally known as the methods used with vegetables. Otherwise there is no reason why a few of each should not be included in every garden of average size. Their requirements are not exacting: the amount of skill, or rather of attention, required to care for them is not more than that required by the ordinary vegetables. In fact, once they are well established they will demand less time than the annual vegetables.

Of these small fruits the most popular and useful are: the strawberry, the blackberry, dewberry and raspberry, the currant, gooseberry and grape.

The strawberry is the most important, and most amateurs attempt its culture—many, however, with indifferent success. This is due, partly at least, to the fact that many methods are advocated by successful growers, and that the beginner is not likely to pick out one and stick to it; and further, that he is led to pay more attention to how many layers he will have, and at what distance he will set the plants, than to proper selection and preparation of soil and other vital matters.

The soil should be well drained and rich—a good garden soil being suitable. The strawberries should not follow sod or corn. If yard manure is used it should be old and well-rotted, so as to be as free as possible from weed seeds. Potash, in some form (see Fertilizers) should be added. The bed should be thoroughly prepared, so that the plants, which need careful transplanting, may take hold at once. A good sunny exposure is preferable, and a spot where no water will collect is essential.

The plants are grown from "layers." They are taken in two ways:

(1) by rooting the runners in the soil; and
(2) by layering in pots.

Grapes are one of the surest and most delicious crops the home garden can grow. The vines are permitted to grow only three or four feet high, then stretched out over wires to get the maximum air and sun

In the former method they are either allowed to root themselves, or, which gives decidedly better results, by selecting vines from strong plants and pushing them lightly down into the soil where the new crown is to be formed. In the second method, two-inch or three-inch pots are used, filling these with soil from the bed and plunging, or burying, them level with the surface, just below where the crown is to be formed, and holding the vine in place with a small stone, which serves the additional purpose of marking where the pot is. In either case these layers are made after the fruiting season.

SETTING THE PLANTS

In using the soil-rooted layers, it is generally more satisfactory to set them out in spring, as soon as the ground can be worked, although they are sometimes set in early fall—August or September—when the ground is in very good condition, so that a good growth can at once be made. Care should be used in transplanting. Have the bed fresh; keep the plants out of the soil as short a time as possible; set the plants in straight, and firm the soil; set just down to the crown—do not cover it. If the soil is dry, or the season late, cut off all old leaves before planting; also shorten back the roots about one-third and be sure not to crowd them when setting, for which purpose a trowel, not a dibble, should be used if the condition of the ground makes the use of any implement necessary. If so dry that water must be used, apply it in the bottom of the hole. If very hot and dry, shade for a day or two.

METHODS OF GROWING

I describe the three systems most valuable for the home garden:

(1) the hill,
(2) the matted row, and
(3) the pot-layered.

(1) In the hill system the plants are put in single rows, or in beds of three or four rows, the plants one foot apart and the rows, or beds, two or three feet apart. In either case each plant is kept separate, and all runners are pinched off as fast as they form, the idea being to throw all the strength into one strong crown.

These currant bushes, though fifteen years old, are kept pruned down to three feet in height. They bear fruits that are as large as cherries

(2) In the matted row system the plants are set in single rows, and the runners set in the bed at five or six inches each side of the plants, and then trained lengthways of the row, this making it a foot or so wide. The runners used to make these secondary crowns must be the first ones sent out by the plants; they should be severed from the parent plants as soon as well rooted. All other runners must be taken off as they form. To keep the beds for a good second crop, where the space between the rows has been kept cultivated and clean, cut out the old plants as soon as the first crop of berries is gathered, leaving the new ones—layered the year before— about one foot apart.

(3) The pot-layering system, especially for a small number of plants, I consider the best. It will be seen that by the above systems the ground is occupied three years, to get two crops, and the strawberry season is a short one at best. By this third system the strawberry is made practically an annual, and the finest of berries are produced. The new plants are layered in pots, as described above. The layers are taken immediately after the fruit is gathered; or better still, because earlier, a few plants are picked out especially to make runners. In either case, fork up the soil about the plants to be layered, and in about fifteen days they will be ready to have the pots placed under them. The main point is to have pot plants ready to go into the new bed as soon as possible after the middle of July. These are set out as in the hill system, and all runners kept pinched off, so that a large crown has been formed by the time the ground freezes, and a full crop of the very best berries will be assured for the following spring. The pot-layering is repeated each year, and the old plants thrown out, no attempt being made to get a second crop. It will be observed that ground is occupied by the strawberries only the latter half of the one season and the beginning of the next, leaving ample time for a crop of early lettuce, cabbage or peas before the plants are set, say in 1911, and for late cabbage or celery after the bed is thrown out, in 1912. Thus the ground is made to yield three crops in two years—a very important point where garden space is limited.

CULTIVATION

Whatever system is used—and each has its advocates—the strawberry bed must be kept clean, and attention given to removing the surplus runners. Cultivate frequently enough to keep a dust mulch between the rows, as advocated for garden crops. At first, after setting, the cultivation may be as deep as three or four inches, but as the roots develop and fill the ground it should be restricted to two inches at most. Where a horse is used a Planet Jr. twelve-tooth cultivator will be just the thing.

MULCHING

After the ground freezes, and before severe cold sets in (about the 1st to the 15th of December) the bed should be given its winter mulch. Bog hay, which may be obtained cheaply from some nearby farmer, is about the best material. Clean straw will do. Cover the entire bed, one or two inches over the plants, and two or three between the rows. If necessary, hold in place with old boards. In spring, but not before the plants begin to grow, over each plant the mulch is pushed aside to let it through. Besides giving winter protection, the mulch acts as a clean even support for the berries and keeps the roots cool and moist.

INSECTS AND DISEASE

For white-grub and cut-worm see pages elsewhere in the text. For rust, which frequently injures the leaves so seriously as to cause practical loss of crop, choose hardy varieties and change bed frequently. Spraying with Bordeaux, 5-5-50, four or five times during first season plants are set, and second season just before and just after blossoming, will prevent it. In making up your strawberry list remember that some varieties have imperfect, or pistillate blossoms, and that when such varieties are used a row of some perfect-flowering (bi- sexual) sort must be set every nine to twelve feet.

VARIETIES

New strawberries are being introduced constantly; also, they vary greatly in their adaptation to locality. Therefore it is difficult to advise as to what varieties to plant. The following, however, have proved satisfactory over wide areas, and may be depended upon to give satisfaction.

- Early crop:—Michel's Early, Haverland, Climax;

- Mid- season crop:—Bubach No. 5, Brandywine, Marshall, Nic. Ohmer, Wm. Belt, Glen Mary, Sharplesss;

- Late crop:—The Gandy, Sample, Lester Lovett.

The blackberry, dewberry and raspberry are all treated in much the same way. The soil should be well drained, but if a little clayey, so much the better. They are planned preferably in early spring, and set from three or four to six or seven feet apart, according to the variety. They should be put in firmly. Set the plants in about as deep as they have been growing, and cut the canes back to six or eight inches. If fruit is wanted the same season as bushes are set, get a few extra plants—they cost but a few cents—and cut back to two feet or so. Plants fruited the first season are not likely to do well the following year. Two plants may be set in a place and one fruited. If this one is exhausted, then little will be lost. Give clean cultivation frequently enough to maintain a soil mulch, as it is very necessary to retain all the moisture possible. Cultivation, though frequent, should be very shallow as soon as the plants get a good start. In very hot seasons, if the ground is clean, a summer mulch of old hay, leaves or rough manure will be good for the same purpose.

In growing, a good stout stake is used for each plant, to which the canes are tied with some soft material. Or, a stout wire is strung the length of the row and the canes fastened to this—a better way, however, being to string two wires, one on either side of the row.

Another very important matter is that of pruning. The plants if left to themselves will throw up altogether too much wood. This must be cut out to four or five of the new canes and all the canes that have borne fruit should be cut and burned each season as soon as through fruiting. The canes, for instance, that grow in 1911 will be those to fruit in 1912, after which they should be immediately removed. The new canes, if they are to be self-supporting, as sometimes grown, should be cut back when three or four feet high.

It is best, however, to give support. In the case of those varieties which make fruiting side-shoots, as most of the black raspberries (blackcaps) do, the canes should be cut back at two to three feet, and it is well also to cut back these side shoots one-third to one-half, early in the spring.

In cold sections (New York or north of it) it is safest to give winter protection by "laying down" the canes and giving them a mulch of rough material. Having them near the ground is in itself a great protection, as they will not be exposed to sun and wind and will sometimes be covered with snow.

For mulching, the canes are bent over nearly at the soil and a shovelful of earth thrown on the tips to hold them down; the entire canes may then be covered with soil or rough manure, but do not put it on until freezing weather is at hand. If a mulch is used, it must be taken off before growth starts in the spring.

THE BLACKBERRY

The large-growing sorts are set as much as six by eight feet apart, though with careful staking and pruning they may be comfortably handled in less space. The smaller sorts need about four by six. When growth starts, thin out to four or five canes and pinch these off at about three feet; or, if they are to be put on wires or trellis, they may be cut when tied up the following spring. Cultivate, mulch and prune as suggested above.

Blackberries will do well on a soil a little dry for raspberries and they do not need it quite so rich, as in this case the canes do not ripen up sufficiently by fall, which is essential for good crops. If growing rank they should be pinched back in late August. When tying up in the spring, the canes should be cut back to four or five feet and the laterals to not more than eighteen inches.

Blackberry enemies do not do extensive injury, as a rule, in well-cared-for beds. The most serious are:

(1) the rust or blight, for which there is no cure but carefully pulling and burning the plants as fast as infested;

(2) the blackberry-bush borer, for which burn infested canes; and

(3) the recently introduced bramble flea-louse, which resembles the green plant-louse or aphis except that it is a brisk jumper, like the flea-beetle.

The leaves twist and curl up in summer and do not drop off in the fall. On cold early mornings, or wet weather, while the insects are sluggish, cut all infested shoots, collecting them in a tight box, and burn.

BLACKBERRY VARIETIES

As with the other small fruits, so many varieties are being introduced that it is difficult to give a list of the best for home use. Any selections from the following, however, will prove satisfactory, as they are tried-and-true:—Early King, Early Harvest, Wilson Junior, Kittatinny, Rathburn, Snyder, Erie.

THE DEWBERRY

This is really a trailing blackberry and needs the same culture, except that the canes are naturally slender and trailing and therefore, for garden culture, must have support. They may be staked up, or a barrel hoop, supported by two stakes, makes a good support. In ripening, the dewberry is ten to fourteen days earlier than the blackberry, and for that reason a few plants should be included in the berry patch. Premo is the earliest sort, and Lucretia the standard.

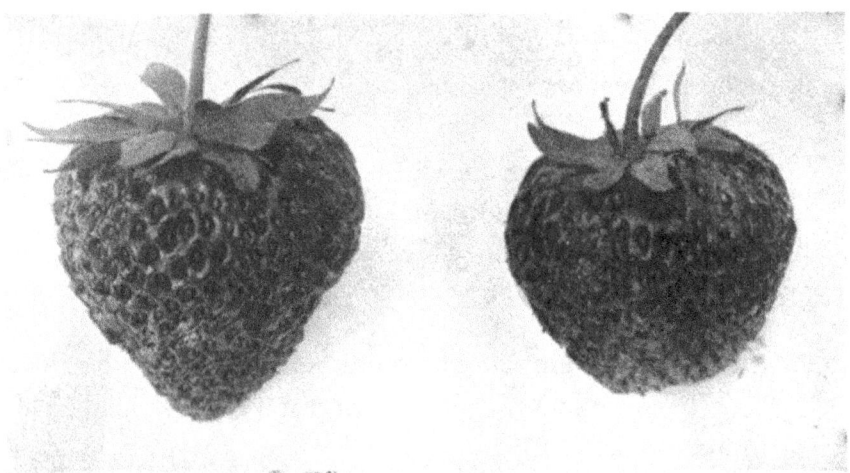

Gandy, one of the best late strawberries   Marshall, a standard main-crop variety

Strawberry plants are propagated by what is called pot-layering. Runners from the old plants are pegged down in pots until they take root and form new plants

RASPBERRY

The black and the red types are distinct in flavor, and both should be grown. The blackcaps need more room, about three by six or seven feet; for the reds three by five feet will be sufficient. The blackcaps, and a few of the reds, like Cuthbert, throw out fruiting side branches, and should have the main canes cut back at about two and a half feet to encourage the growth of these laterals, which, in the following spring, should be cut back to about one-third their length. The soil for raspberries should be clayey if possible, and moist, but not wet.

RASPBERRY ENEMIES

The orange rust, which attacks the blackberry also, is a serious trouble. Pull up and burn all infested plants at once, as no good remedy has as yet been found. The cut-worm, especially in newly set beds, may sometimes prove destructive of the sprouting young canes. The raspberry-borer is the larva of a small, flattish, red-necked beetle, which bores to the center of the canes during summer growth, and kills them. Cut and burn.

RASPBERRY VARIETIES

Of the blackcaps, Gregg, McCormick, Munger, Cumberland, Columbian, Palmer (very early), and Eureka (late), are all good sorts. Reds: Cuthbert, Cardinal (new), Turner, Reliance, The King (extra early), Loudon (late). Yellow: Golden Queen.

CURRANTS

The currant and gooseberry are very similar in their cultural requirements. A deep, rich and moist soil is the best—approaching a clayey loam. There need be no fear of giving too much manure, but it should be well rotted. Plenty of room, plenty of air, plenty of moisture, secured where necessary by a soil or other mulch in hot dry weather, are essential to the production of the best fruit.

The currant will stand probably as much abuse as any plant the home gardener will have to deal with. Stuck in a corner, smothered in sod, crowded with old wood, stripped by the currant-worm, it still struggles along from year to year, ever hopefully trying to produce a meager crop of poor fruit. But these are not the sort you want. Although it is so tough, no fruit will respond to good care more quickly.

To have it do well, give it room, four or five feet each way between bushes. Manure it liberally; give it clean cultivation, and as the season gets hot and dry, mulch the soil, if you would be certain of a full-sized, full-flavored crop. Two bushes, well cared for, will yield more than a dozen half-neglected ones. Anywhere north of New York a full crop every year may be made almost certain.

PRUNING CURRANTS

Besides careful cultivation, to insure the best of fruit it is necessary to give some thought to the matter of pruning. The most convenient and the most satisfactory way is to keep it in the bush form. Set the plants singly, three or four feet apart, and so cut the new growth, which is generously produced, as to retain a uniform bush shape, preferably rather open in the center.

The fruit is produced on wood two or more years old. Therefore cut out branches either when very small, or not until four or five years later, after it has borne two or three crops of fruit. Therefore, in pruning currants, take out

1. superfluous young growth;

2. old hard wood (as new wood will produce better fruit); and

3. all weak, broken, dead or diseased shoots;

4. during summer, if the tips of the young growths kept for fruiting are pinched off, they will ripen up much better— meaning better fruit when they bear;

5. to maintain a good form, the whole plant may be cut back (never more than one-third) in the fall.

In special situations it may be advisable to train the currant to one or a few main stems, as against a wall; this can be done, but it is less convenient. Also it brings greater danger from the currant-borer.

The black currant, used almost entirely for culinary or preserving purposes, is entirely different from the red and white ones. They are much larger and should be put five to six feet apart. Some of the fruit is borne on one-year-old wood, so the shoots should not be cut back. Moreover, old wood bears as good fruit as the new growth, and need not be cut out, unless the plant is getting crowded, for several years. As the wood is much heavier and stronger than the other currants, it is advisable gradually to develop the black currants into the tree form.

Grow your own currants for the table and particularly for jelly making

Blackberries of quality are one of the most satisfactory breakfast-table fruits

For what you would pay for these you could buy a dozen good raspberry plants—enough with a little care to yield several dozen boxes of fine fruit the following season

Gooseberries like these may be grown in every garden. With the advent of modern sprays the dreaded mildew may be held in check

ENEMIES OF THE CURRANT

The worst of these is the common currant-worm. When he appears, which will be indicated by holes eaten in the lower leaves early in spring, generally before the plants bloom, spray at once with Paris green. If a second brood appears, spray with white hellebore (if this is not all washed off by the rain, wipe from the fruit when gathered). For the borer, cut and burn every infested shoot. Examine the bushes in late fall, and those in which the borers are at work will usually have a wilted appearance and be of a brownish color.

VARIETIES OF CURRANTS

Red Dutch, while older and smaller than some of the newer varieties, is hardier and not so likely to be hurt by the borer. London Market, Fay's Prolific, Perfection (new), and Prince Albert, are good sorts. White Grape is a good white. Naples, and Lee's Prolific are good black sorts.

THE GOOSEBERRY

This is given practically the same treatment as the currant. It is even more important that it should be given the coolest, airiest, location possible, and the most moist soil. Even a partially shaded situation will do, but in such situations extra care must be taken to guard against the mildew—which is mentioned below. Summer mulching is, of course, of special benefit.

In pruning the gooseberry, it is best to cut out to a very few, or even to a single stem. Keep the head open, to allow free circulation of air. The extent of pruning will make a great difference in the size of the fruit; if fruit of the largest size is wanted, prune very close. All branches drooping to the ground should be removed. Keep the branches, as much as possible, from touching each other.

GOOSEBERRY ENEMIES

The currant-worm attacks the gooseberry also, and is effectively handled by the arsenate of lead, Paris green or hellebore spraying, mentioned above.

The great trouble in growing gooseberries successfully is the powdery mildew—a dirty, whitish fungous growth covering both fruit and leaves. It is especially destructive of the foreign varieties, the culture of which, until the advent of the potassium sulfide spray, was being practically abandoned. Use 1 oz. of potassium sulfide (liver of sulphur) to 2 gals. water, and mix just before using. Spray thoroughly three or four times a month, from the time the blossoms are opening until fruit is ripe.

GOOSEBERRY VARIETIES

Of the native gooseberries—which are the hardiest, Downing and Houghton's Seedling are most used. Industry is an English variety, doing well here. Golden Prolific, Champion, and Columbus, are other good foreign sorts, but only when the mildew is successfully fought off.

THE GRAPE

No garden is so small that there cannot be found in it room for three or four grape-vines; no fruit is more certain, and few more delicious.

If it is convenient, a situation fully exposed to the sun, and sloping slightly, will be preferable. But any good soil, provided only it is rich and thoroughly drained, will produce good results. If a few vines are to be set against walls, or in other out-of-the-way places, prepare the ground for them by excavating a good-sized hole, putting in a foot of coal cinders or other drainage material, and refilling with good heavy loam, enriched with old, well-rotted manure and half a peck of wood ashes. For culture in the garden, such special preparation will not be necessary—although, if the soil is not in good shape, it will be advisable slightly to enrich the hills.

One or two-year roots will be the most satisfactory to buy. They may be set in either fall or spring—the latter time, for New York or north, being generally preferable. When planting, the cane should be cut back to three or four eyes, and the roots should also be shortened back— usually about one-third. Be sure to make the hole large enough, when setting, to let the roots spread naturally, and work the soil in well around them with the fingers. Set them in firmly, by pressing down hard with the ball of the foot after firming by hand. They are set about six feet apart.

GRAPE PRUNING

As stated above, the vine is cut back, when planting, to three or four eyes. The subsequent pruning—and the reader must at once distinguish between pruning, and training, or the way in which the vines are placed—will determine more than anything else the success of the undertaking. Grapes depend more upon proper pruning than any other fruit or vegetable in the garden. Two principles must be kept track of in this work. First principle: the annual crop is borne only on canes of the same year's growth, springing from wood of the previous season's growth. Second principle: the vine, if left to itself, will set three or four times the number of bunches it can properly mature. As a result of these facts, the following system of pruning has been developed and must be followed for sure and full-sized crops.

1. At time of planting, cut back to three or four eyes, and after these sprout leave only one (or two) of them, which should be staked up.

2. Following winter (December to March), leave only one cane and cut this back to three or four eyes.

3. Second growing season, save only two canes, even if several sprout, and train these to stake or trellis. These two vines, or arms, branching from the main stem, form the foundation for the one-year canes that bear the fruit. However, to prevent the vine's setting too much fruit (see second principle above) these arms must be cut back in order to limit the number of fruit-bearing canes that will spring from them, therefore:

4. Second winter pruning, cut back these arms to eight or ten buds— and we have prepared for the first crop of fruit, about forty bunches, as the fruiting cane from each bud will bear two bunches on the average. However these main arms will not bear fruiting-canes another year (see first principle above) and therefore:

At the third winter pruning,

a. of the canes that bore fruit, only the three or four nearest the main stem or trunk are left;

b. these are cut back to eight or ten buds each, and

c. everything else is ruthlessly cut away.

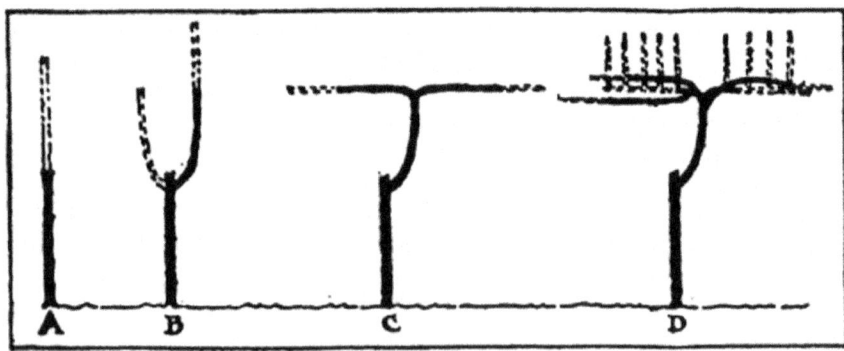

Each succeeding year the same system is continued, care being taken to rub off, each May, buds or sprouts starting on the main trunk or arms.

The wood, in addition to being cut back, must be well ripened; and the wood does not ripen until after the fruit. It therefore sometimes becomes necessary to cut out some of the bunches in order to hasten the ripening of the rest. At the same time the application of some potash fertilizer will be helpful. If the bunches do not ripen up quickly and pretty nearly together, the vine is overloaded and being damaged for the following year.

The matter of pruning being mastered, the question of training is one of individual choice. Poles, trellises, arbors, walls—almost anything may be used. The most convenient system, however, and the one I would strongly recommend for practical home gardening for results, is known as the (modified) Kniffen system. It is simplicity itself. A stout wire is stretched five or six feet above the ground; to this the single main trunks of the vine run up, and along it are stretched the two or three arms from which the fruiting-canes hang down. They occupy the least possible space, so that garden crops may be grown practically on the same ground. I have never seen it tried, but where garden space is limited I should think that the asparagus bed and the Kniffen grape- arbor just described could be combined to great advantage by placing the vines, in spaces left for them, directly in the asparagus row. Of course the ground would have to be manured for two crops. A 2-8-10 fertilizer is right for the grapes. If using stable manure, apply also ashes or some other potash fertilizer.

If the old-fashioned arbor is used, the best way is to run the main trunk up over it and cut the laterals back each year to two or three eyes.

The most serious grape trouble which the home gardener is likely to encounter is the black-rot Where only a few grapes are grown the simplest way of overcoming this disease is to get a few dozen cheap manila store-bags and fasten one, with a couple of ten-penny nails, over each bunch. Cut the mouth of the bag at sides and edges, cover the bunch, fold the flaps formed over the cane, and fasten. They are put on after the bunches are well formed and hasten the ripening of the fruit, as well as protecting it. On a larger scale, spraying will have to be resorted to. Use Bordeaux, 5-5-50, from third leaf's appearance to middle of July; balance of season with ammoniacal copper carbonate. The spray should be applied in particular just before every rain— especially on the season's growth. Besides the spraying, all trimmed- off wood, old leaves and twigs, withered bunches and grapes, or "mummies," and refuse of every description, should be carefully raked up in the spring and burned or buried. Also give clean culture and keep the main stems clean.

The grape completes the list of the small fruits worthwhile to the average home gardener. If you have not already experimented with them, do not let your garden go longer without them. They are all easily obtained (none costing more than a few cents each), and a very limited number will keep the family table well supplied with healthy delicacies, which otherwise, in their best varieties and condition, could not be had at all. The various operations of setting out, pruning and spraying will soon become as familiar as those in the vegetable garden. There is no reason why every home garden should not have its few rows of small fruits, yielding their delicious harvests in abundance.

Chapter 19

A Calendar of Operations

One of the greatest difficulties in gardening is to get things started ahead at the proper time, and yet upon the thoroughness with which this is done the success of the garden must depend, in large measure.

The reader may remember that in a previous chapter (Chapter IV) the importance of accurately planning the work ahead was emphasized. I mentioned there the check list used to make sure that everything would be carried out, or started ahead at the proper time—as with the sowing of seeds. The following garden operations, given month by month, will serve not only as a timely reminder of things to be done, but as the basis for such a check list. The importance of the preparations in all matters of gardening, is of course obvious.

JANUARY

Probably one of the good resolutions made with the New Year was a better garden for the coming summer. The psychologists claim that the only hope for resolutions is to nail them down at the start with an action—that seems to have more effect in making an actual impression on the brain. So start the good work along by sending at once for several of the leading seed catalogues.

Planting Plan. Make out a list of what you are going to want this year, and then make your Planting Plan. See Chapter IV.

Seeds. Order your seed. Do it now while the seedsman's stock is full; while he is not rushed; while there is ample time to rectify mistakes if any occur.

Manures. Altogether too few amateur gardeners realize the great importance of procuring early every pound of manures, of any kind, to be had. It often may be had cheaply at this time of year, and by composting, adding phosphate rock, and several turnings, if you have any place under cover where it can be collected, you can double its value before spring.

Frames. Even at this season of the year do not fail to air the frames well on warm days. Practically no water will be needed, but if the soil does dry out sufficiently to need it, apply early on a bright morning.

Onions. It will not be too early, this month, to sow onions for spring transplanting outside. Get a packet each of Prizetaker, Ailsa Craig, Mammoth Silver-skin, or Gigantic Gibraltar.

Lettuce. Sow lettuce for spring crop under glass or in frames.

Fruit. This is a good month to prune grapes, currants, gooseberries and peach trees, to avoid the rush that will come later.

FEBRUARY

Hotbeds. A little early for making them until after the 15th, but get all your material ready—manure, selected and stacked; lumber ready for any new ones; sash all in good repair.

Starting Seeds. First part of the month, earliest planting of cabbage, cauliflower and lettuce should be made; and two to four weeks later for main early crop. At this time also, beets and earliest celery.

Tools. Overhaul them all now; order repairs. Get new catalogues and study new improvements and kinds you do not possess.

Poles and brush. Whether you use the old-fashioned sort (now harder to obtain than they used to be) or make your "poles" and use wire trellis for peas, attend to it now.

Fruit. Finish up last month's work, if not all done. Also examine plum and cherry trees for black-knot.

MARCH

Hotbeds. If not made last of February, should be made at once. Some of the seed sown last month will be ready for transplanting and going into the frames; also lettuce sown in January. Radish and carrot (forcing varieties) may be sown in alternating rows. Give much more air; water on bright mornings; be careful not to have them caught by suddenly cold nights after a bright warm day.

Seed-sowing under glass. Last sowing of early cabbage and early summer cabbages (like Succession), lettuce, rhubarb (for seedling plants), cauliflower, radish, spinach, turnip, and early tomatoes; towards last of month, late tomatoes and first of peppers, and egg- plant. Sweet peas often find a place in the vegetable garden; start a few early, to set out later; they will do better than if started outside. Start tomatoes for growing in frames. For early potatoes sprout in sand.

Planting, outside. If an early spring, and the ground is sufficiently dry, sow onions, lettuce, beet, radish, (sweet peas), smooth peas, early carrot, cabbage, leek, celery (main crop), and turnip. Set out new beds of asparagus, rhubarb and sea-kale (be sure to try a few plants of the latter). Manure and fork up old beds of above.

Fruit. Prune now, apple, plum and pear trees. And this is the last chance for lime-sulphur and miscible-oil sprays.

APRIL

Now the rush is on! Plan your work, and work your plan. But do not yield to the temptation to plant more than you can look out for later on. Remember it is much easier to sow seeds than to pull out weeds.

The Frames. Air! water! and do not let the green plant-lice or the white-fly get a ghost of a chance to start. Almost every day the glass should be lifted entirely off. Care must be taken never to let the soil or flats become dried out; toward the end of the month, if it is bright and warm, begin watering towards evening instead of in early morning, as you should have been doing through the winter. If proper attention is given to ventilation and moisture, there will not be much danger from the green plant-louse (aphis) and white-fly, but at the first sign of one fight them to a finish. Use kerosene emulsion, tobacco dust, tobacco preparations, or Aphine.

Seed sowing. Under glass: tomato, egg-plant and peppers. On sod: corn, cucumbers, melons, early squash, lima beans.

Planting, outside. Onions, lettuce, beet, etc., if not put in last month; also parsnip, salsify, parsley, wrinkled peas, endive. Toward the end of this month (or first part of next) second plantings of these. Set out plants of early cabbage (and the cabbage group) lettuce, onion sets, sprouted potatoes, beets, etc.

In the Garden. Cultivate between rows of sowed crops; weed out by hand just as soon as they are up enough to be seen; watch for cut-worms and root-maggots.

Fruit. Thin out all old blackberry canes, dewberry and raspberry canes (if this was not done, as it should have been, directly after the fruiting season last summer). Be ready for first spraying of early- blossoming trees. Set out new strawberry beds, small fruits and fruit trees.

MAY

Keep ahead of the weeds. This is the month when those warm, south, driving rains often keep the ground too wet to work for days at a time, and weeds grow by leaps and bounds. Woe betide the gardener whose rows of sprouting onions, beets, carrots, etc., once become green with wild turnip and other rapid-growing intruders. Clean cultivation and slight hilling of plants set out are also essential.

The Frames. These will not need so much attention now, but care must be taken to guard tender plants, such as tomatoes, egg-plant and peppers, against sudden late frosts. The sash may be left off most of the time. Water copiously and often.

Planting, outside. First part of the month: early beans, early corn, okra and late potatoes may be put in; and first tomatoes set out —even if a few are lost—they are readily replaced. Finish setting out cabbage, lettuce, cauliflower, beets, etc., from frames. Latter part of month, if warm: corn, cucumbers, some of sods from frames and early squash as traps where late crop is to be planted or set.

Fruit. Be on time with first sprayings of late-blossoming fruits—apples, etc. Rub off from grape vines the shoots that are not wanted.

JUNE

Frequent, shallow cultivation!

Firm seeds in dry soil. Plant wax beans, lima beans, pole beans, melons, corn, etc., and successive crops of lettuce, radish, etc.

Top-dress growing crops that need special manure (such as nitrate of soda on onions). Prune tomatoes, and cut out some foliage for extra early tomatoes. Toward end of month set celery and late cabbage. Also sow beans, beets, corn, etc., for early fall crops. Spray where necessary. Allow asparagus to grow to tops.

Fruit. Attend to spraying fruit trees and currants and gooseberries. Make pot-layers of strawberries for July setting.

JULY

Maintain frequent, shallow cultivation. Set out late cabbage, cauliflower, broccoli, leeks and celery. Sow beans, beets, corn, etc., for late fall crops. Irrigate where needed.

Fruit. Pinch back new canes of blackberry, dewberry and raspberry. Rub off second crop of buds on grapes. Thin out if too many bunches; also on plums, peaches and other fruit too thick, or touching. Pot-layered strawberries may be set out.

AUGUST

Keep the garden clean from late weeds—especially purslane, the hot-weather weed pest, which should be always removed from the garden and burned or rotted down.

Sow spinach, rutabaga turnip, bush beans and peas for last fall crop. During first part of month, late celery may still be put out. Sow lettuce for early fall crop, in frames. First lot of endive should be tied up for blanching.

Fruit. Strawberries may be set, and pot-layered plants, if wanted to bear a full crop the following season, should be put in by the Thin out and bag grapes.

SEPTEMBER

Frames. Set in lettuce started in August. Sow radishes and successive crop of lettuce. Cooler weather begins to tell on late- planted crops. Give cabbage, cauliflower, etc., deeper cultivation. "Handle" celery wanted for early use.

Harvest and store onions. Get squash under cover before frost. From the 15th to 25th sow spinach, onions, borecole for wintering over. Sow down thickly to rye all plots as fast as cleared of summer crops; or plow heavy land in ridges. Attend to draining.

Fruit. Trees may be set. Procure barrels for storing fruit in winter. At harvest time it is often impossible to get them at any price.

OCTOBER

Get ready for winter. Blanch rest of endive. Bank celery, to be used before Christmas, where it is. Gather tomatoes, melons, etc., to keep as long as possible. Keep especially clean and well cultivated all crops to be wintered over. Late in the month store cabbage and cauliflower; also beets, carrots, and other root crops. Get boxes, barrels, bins, sand or sphagnum moss ready beforehand, to save time in packing.

Clean the garden; store poles, etc., worth keeping over; burn everything else that will not rot; and compost everything that will.

Fruit. Harvest apples, etc. Pick winter pears just before hard frosts, and store in dry dark place.

NOVEMBER

Frames. Make deep hotbeds for winter lettuce and radishes. Construct frames for use next spring. See that vegetables in cellar, bins, and sheds are safe from freezing. Trench or store celery for spring use. Take in balance of all root crops if any remain in the ground, except, of course, parsnip and salsify for spring use. Put rough manure on asparagus and rhubarb beds. Get mulch ready for spinach, etc., to be wintered over, if they occupy exposed locations.

Fruit. Obtain marsh or salt hay for mulching strawberries. Cut out old wood of cane-fruits—blackberries, etc., if not done after gathering fruit. Look over fruit trees for borers.

DECEMBER

Cover celery stored last month, if trenched out-of-doors. Use only light, loose material at first, gradually covering for winter. Put mulch on spinach, etc.

Fruit. Mulch strawberries. Prune grape-vines; make first application of winter sprays for fruit trees.

AND THEN

set about procuring manures of all kinds from every available source. Remember that anything which will rot will add to the value of your manure pile. Muck, lime, old plastering, sods, weeds (earth and all), street, stable and yard sweepings—all these and numerous others will increase your garden successes of next year.

Chapter 20

Conclusion

It is with a feeling in which there is something of fear that I close these pages—fear that many of those little things which become second nature to the grower of plants and seem unimportant, but which sometimes are just the things that the beginner wants to know about, may have been inadvertently left out. In every operation described, however, I have tried to mention all necessary details. I would urge the reader, nevertheless, to study as thoroughly as possible all the garden problems with which he will find himself confronted and to this end recommend that he read several of the many garden books which are now to be had. It must be to his advantage to see even the same subjects presented again from other points of view. The more familiar he can make himself, both in theory and in practice, with all the multitude of operations which modern gardening involves, the greater success will he attain.

Personally, the further I have gone into the growing of things—and that has now become my business as well as my pleasure—the more absorbingly interesting I find it. Each season, each crop, offers its own problems and a reward for the correct solution of them. It is a work which, even to the beginner, presents the opportunity of deducting new conclusions, trying new experiments, making new discoveries. It is a work which offers pleasant and healthy recreation to the many whose days must be, for the most part, spent in office or shop; and it gives very substantial help in the world-old problem of making both ends meet.

Let the garden beginner be not disappointed if he does not succeed, for the first season or two, or possibly three, with everything he plants. There is usually a preventable reason for the failure, and studious observation will reveal it. With the modern success in the application of insecticides and fungicides, and the extension of the practice of irrigation, the subject of gardening begins to be reduced to a scientific and (what is more to the point) a sure basis. We are getting control of the uncertain factors. All this affects first, perhaps, the person who grows for profit, but with our present wide circulation of every new idea and discovery in such matters, it must reach soon to every remote home garden patch which is cared for by a wide-awake gardener.

Such a person, from the fact that he or she is reading a new garden book, I take the reader to be. I hope this volume, condensed though it is, has added to your fund of practical garden information; that it will help to grow that proverbial second blade of grass. I have only to add, as I turn again to the problems waiting for me in field and under glass, that I wish you all success in your work—the making of better gardens in America.

www.ingramcontent.com/pod-product-compliance
Lightning Source LLC
Chambersburg PA
CBHW070054080526
44586CB00013B/1051